Good
START WITH
Gratitutde

Diana Playa

A guided journal to your best self

Good days
START WITH
Gratitutde

This journal belongs to

_____

"It is not happiness that brings us gratitude. It is gratitude that brings us happiness."

Instructions to the reader

The questions asked in this book will prompt you to address past experiences in your life, talk about people who are no longer with you, and perhaps re-visit wounds that you have not yet healed from. Please feel under no obligation to answer the questions that you are not yet ready to. Skip them, and return back to them when you feel that you are ready, the book will be here whenever you decide that time comes. Allow yourself to be honest and open-minded as your mind will allow you to do so many things, the same way it will stop you. When you have those doubtful thoughts, laugh at them. You are more powerful than your mind and more capable than you believe. With that understanding and this book, it will allow you to become the most grateful version of yourself, and subsequently the happiest.

"You have power over your mind, not outside events. Realise this, and you will find strength."

MARCUS ARELIUS

What is gratitude?

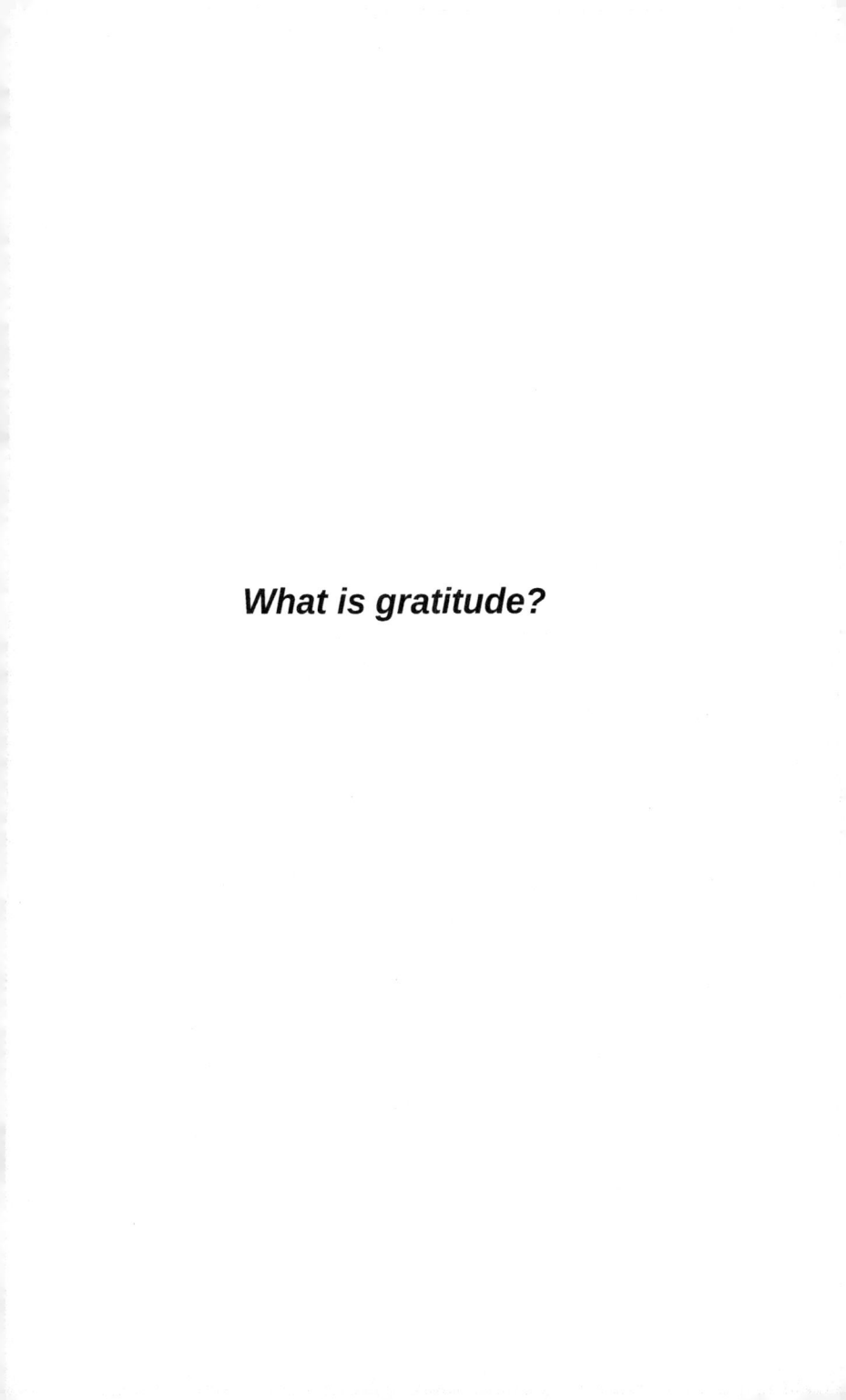

Gratitude meaning

- the quality of being thankful; readiness to show appreciation for and to return kindness.

Gratitude is a way for people to appreciate what they have instead of always reaching for something new in hopes it will make them happier or thinking they can't feel satisfied until every physical and material need is met. Gratitude helps people refocus on what they have instead of what they lack. And, although it may feel contrived at first, this mental state grows stronger with use and practice.

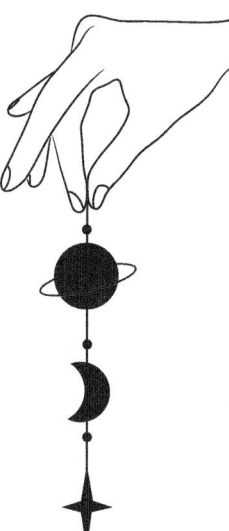

Why is gratitude so important in improving the quality of your life?

In positive psychology research, gratitude is strongly and consistently associated with greater happiness. Gratitude helps people feel more positive emotions, relish good experiences, improve their health, deal with adversity, and build strong relationships. Studies show that those who live there lives with a grateful positive attitude for life, have a much more enjoyable and abundant life in comparison to those who live oppositely.

Many of us express gratitude by saying "thank you" to someone who has helped us or given us a gift. From a scientific perspective, however, gratitude is not just an action: it is also a positive emotion that serves a biological purpose. Positive psychology defines gratitude in a way where scientists can measure its effects, and thus argue that gratitude is more than feeling thankful: it is a deeper appreciation for someone (or something) that produces longer lasting positivity.

And so we begin on our journeys of being our most grateful selves and in turn our best selves

"Appreciation is a wonderful thing. It makes what is excellent in others belong to us as well."

VOLTAIRE

3 things I am grateful to have

1. ....
2. ....
3. ....

3 reasons today was a good day

1. ....
2. ....
3. ....

Draw something that you are grateful for

Today I ate

_____

Tick the elements that you enjoyed the most

◯ **Tasty** ◯ **Reenergising**

◯ **Healthy** ◯ **Filling**

◯ **Enjoyment** ◯ **Flavourful**

◯ **Fresh** ◯ **Homemade**

Why it's important to surround yourself with those who are grateful

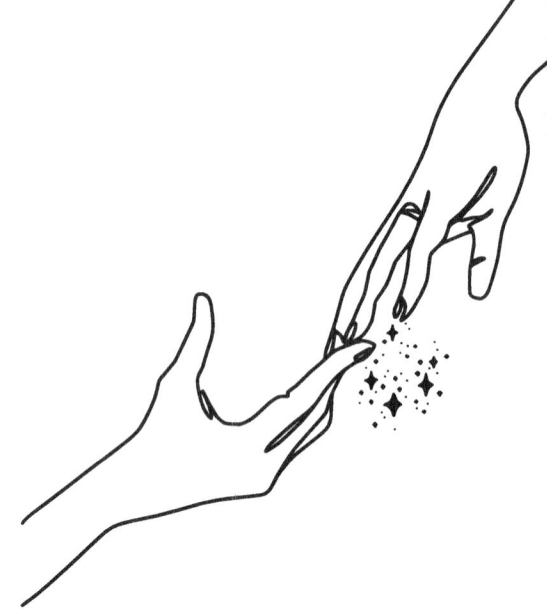

"You cannot hang out with negative people and expect to live a positive life."

Darren Hardy

Emotion is just as infectious as any other transmittable disease. Jim Rohn has once said that "You are the average of the five people you spend most of your time with". Ask yourself, is who you spend most of your time with who you want to become? Because a year from now, who you will be will look a great reflection of exactly who you hang around with now. "If you have a friend whose friendship you wouldn't recommend to your sister, or your father, or your son, why would you have such a friend for yourself?" -Jordan B. Peterson

The Social Proximity Effect

Humans are social creatures and we're all highly influenced by the people around us each day. The Social Proximity Effect Turns You Into Your Friends. You'll mirror the habits of the people you spend most of your time with. Say you don't drink. You go to dinner with 5 of your friends every Saturday who do you drink, perhaps not right away, but in time 5 friends who drink every Saturday at dinner, will become 6 friends who drink every Saturday at dinner. You may even begin to drink when you are not around your friends as you enjoy it so much when you do drink with them. Now you're a casual drinker, like most of your friends. Don't underestimate the power of influence and the need that the majority of humans want to be a part of everything that seems to be fun; due to serious FOMO, (Fear of missing out). It doesn't take long for the proximity effect to start working its way into your behaviour.

The psychological influence of the people you're close to is strong. Just look at you and your best/closest friend. You probably influence a lot of each other's decisions, if not all. Like the type of music you listen to, the way you dress, the way you speak, the good and bad habits you both have. The closer you become to someone, the more your mirror their behaviour and vice versa. Writer Tyler Tervooren addresses something important to keep in mind. The Proximity Effect is not just something to be wary of, and you can also harness it to improve your life.

To build good habits, spend more time with the people who already practice them. If hanging around people with bad habits will cause you to develop bad habits yourself, then the opposite is also true: spending time around people with good habits will cause you to develop good habits. If you're a timid person, it's probably because you spend the bulk of your time with others who mirror that same personality trait. If you want to be more adventurous, find adventurous people to hang out with. Go to a rock climbing gym or find an outdoor-oriented group to join. Want to start a business? It'll be hard to do from inside a cubicle surrounded by other people in other cubicles. To improve your odds of actually starting, find a friend who's already done it.

Search your city for a local entrepreneurs get-together. If you have horrible eating habits and you don't exercise, you might have a circle of friends or relatives that are the same. To change that, you have to change the amount of time you spend with that group and find another set of friends that eat well and do exercise. Opportunities to find people like this are easier than you think. In many cases, you hardly need to worry about doing the actual thing you want to do. Instead, focus your effort on finding people who already do that thing and build relationships with them. Thanks to the social proximity effect, that thing will most likely become a regular part of your life.

"Your level of talent and "potential" are irrelevant if you're surrounded by people who don't help you realize it."

Benjamin P. Hardy

Remembering people from our past can be a joyful experience. It can also be a rather daunting one if that person hurt us in any way. In the next few pages I will prompt you to write about those you are grateful for both presently in your life and no longer in your life. Hopefully this allows you some insight into how your relationships have affected you today, and how you truly feel about them.

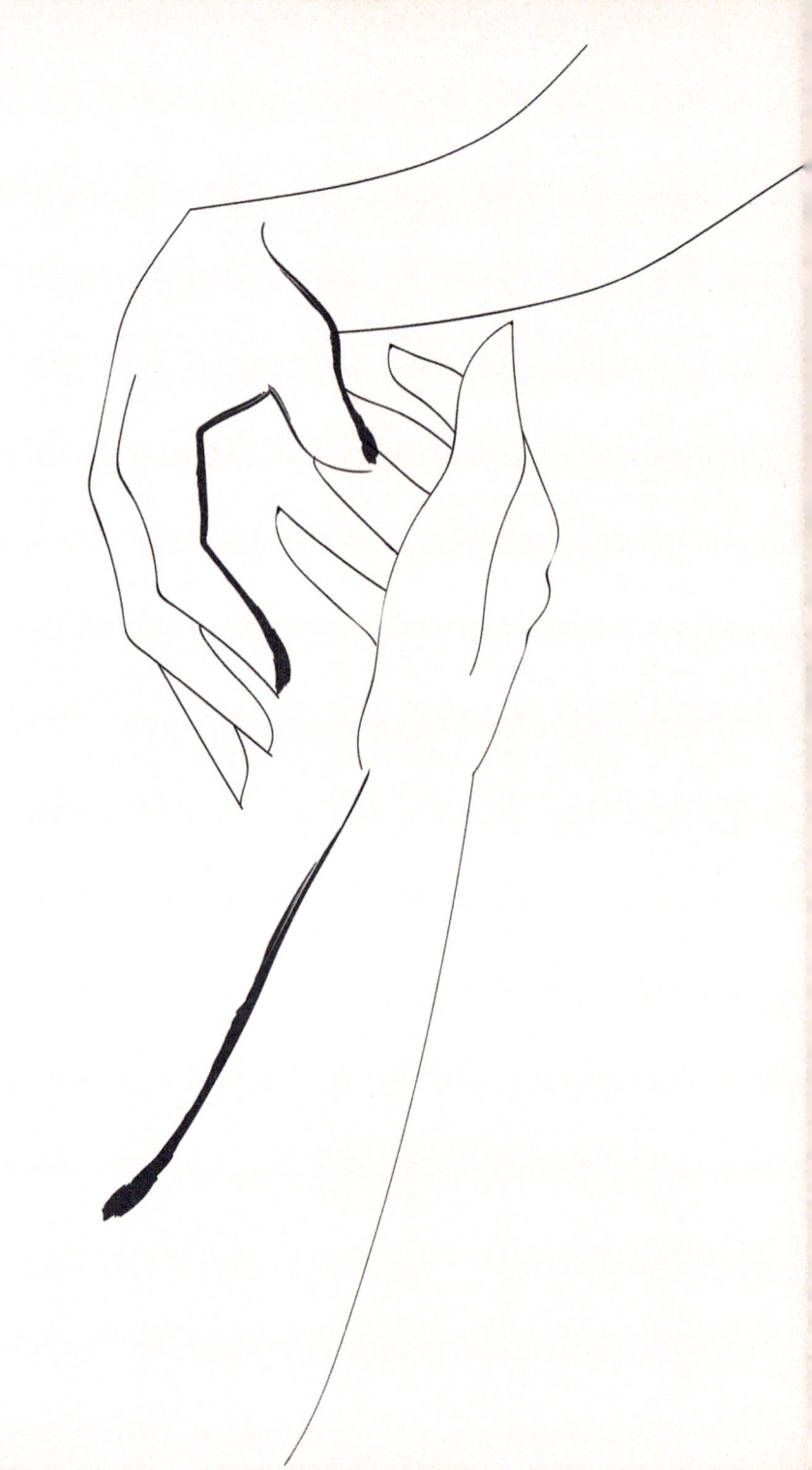

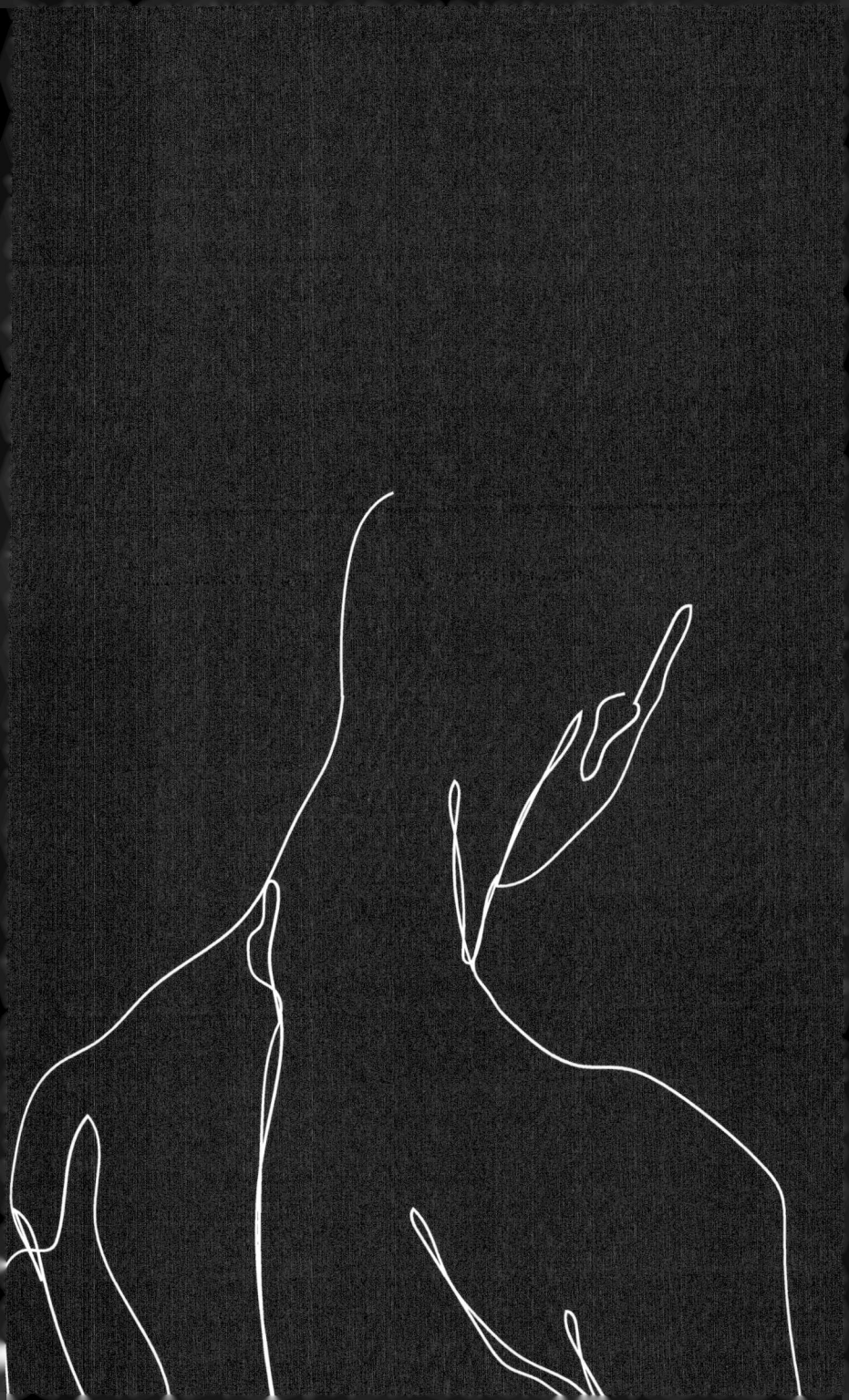

One person in my life who I am grateful for is

———————

I am grateful for this person because

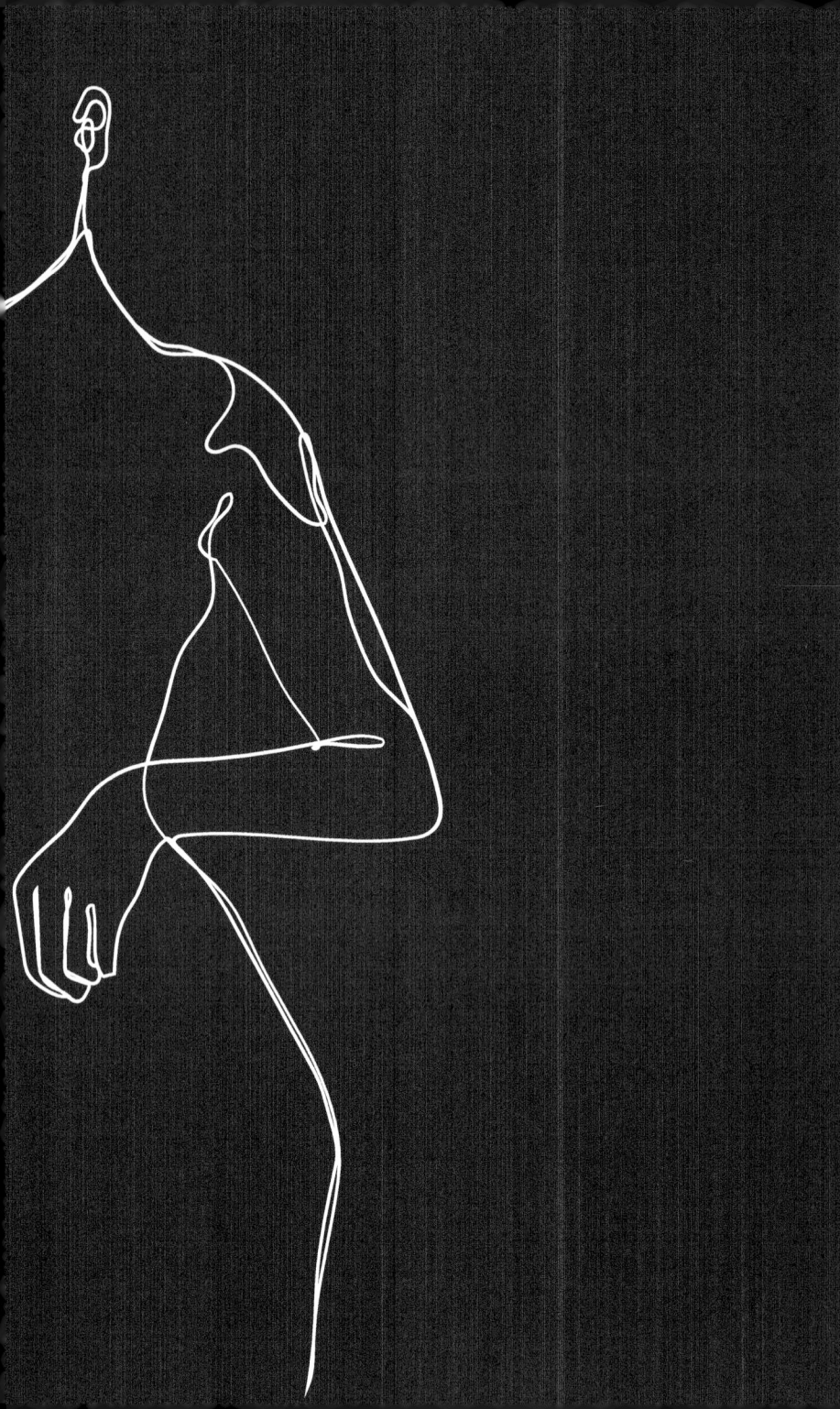

One person who is no longer in my life who I am grateful for is

———————

I am grateful for this person because

3 reasons why I love my friends

1. ....
2. ....
3. ....

3 qualities I love about myself

1. ....
2. ....
3. ....

Draw something that you are grateful for

The Benefits of a Gratitude Journal

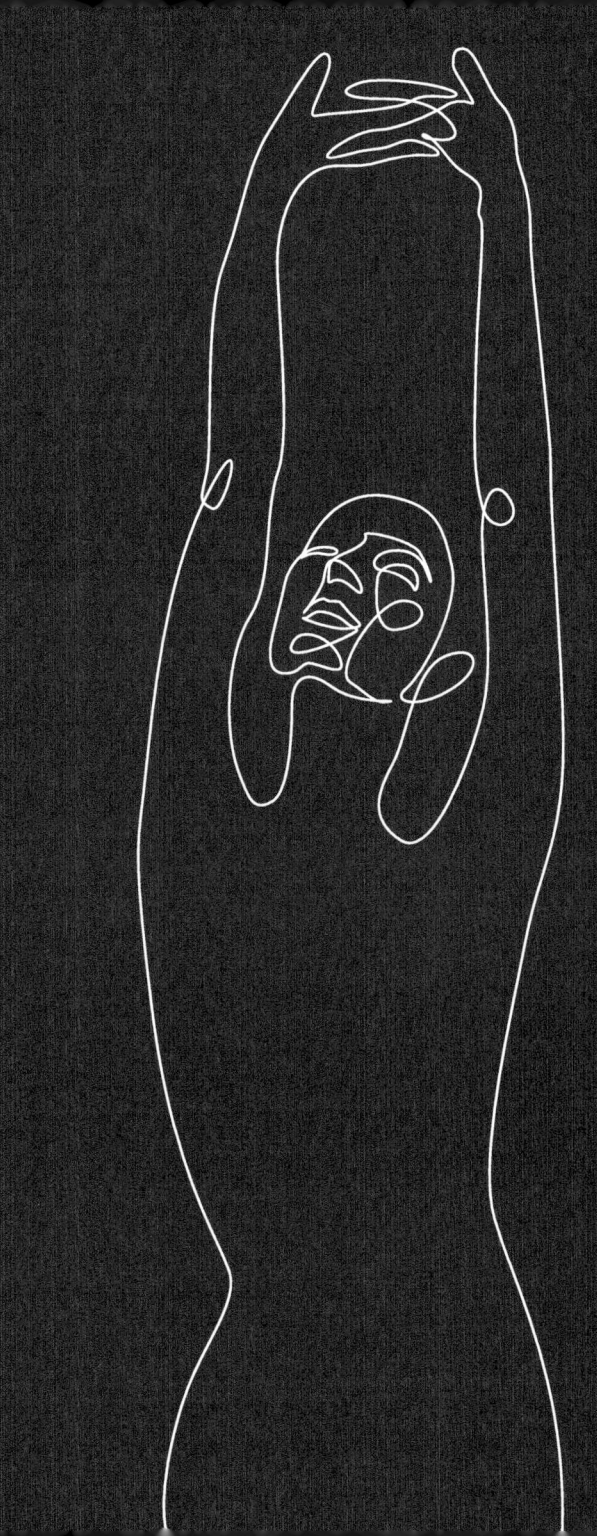

"It's a funny thing about life, once you begin to take note of the things you are grateful for, you begin to lose sight of the things that you lack."

GERMANY KENT

Gratitude journaling is known to be extremely beneficial for the mind

Here are few benefits people have noticed when practicing gratitude journaling in particular

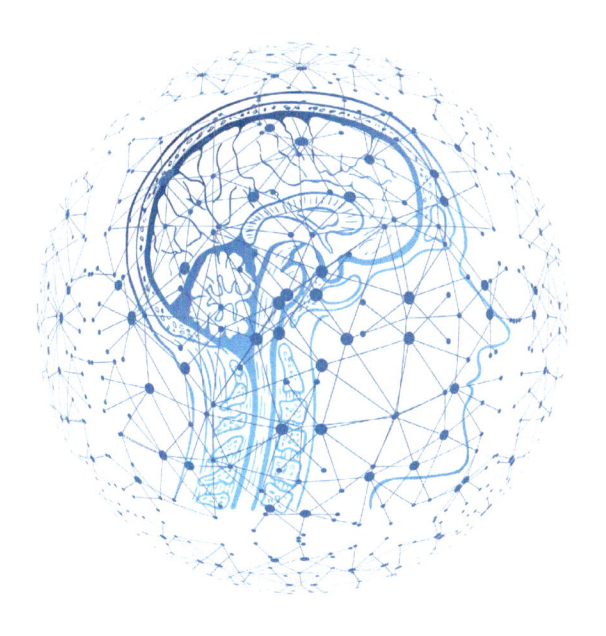

- *Journaling can give you a new perspective on what is important to you and what you truly appreciate in your life*

- *Gratitude journaling, like many gratitude practices, can lower your stress levels*

- *It can help you feel calmer, especially at night*

- *By noting what you are grateful for, you can gain clarity on what you want to have more of in your life, and what you can do without*

- *Gratitude journaling can help you find out and focus on what really matters to you*

- *Keeping a gratitude journal helps you learn more about yourself and become more self-aware*

- *Your gratitude journal is for your eyes only, so you can write anything you feel without worrying about judgment from others*

This week I am grateful for

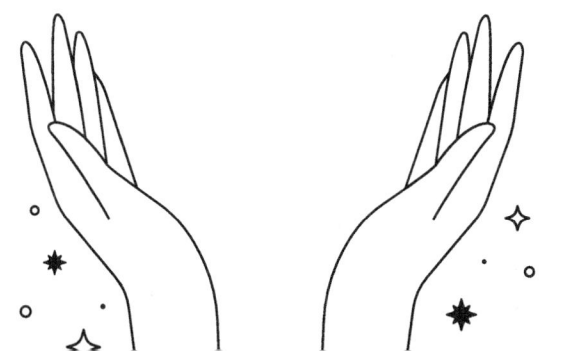

How we are aligned in the universe when we live a life full of gratitude

VS

How we are aligned in the universe when we live a life full of ingratitude

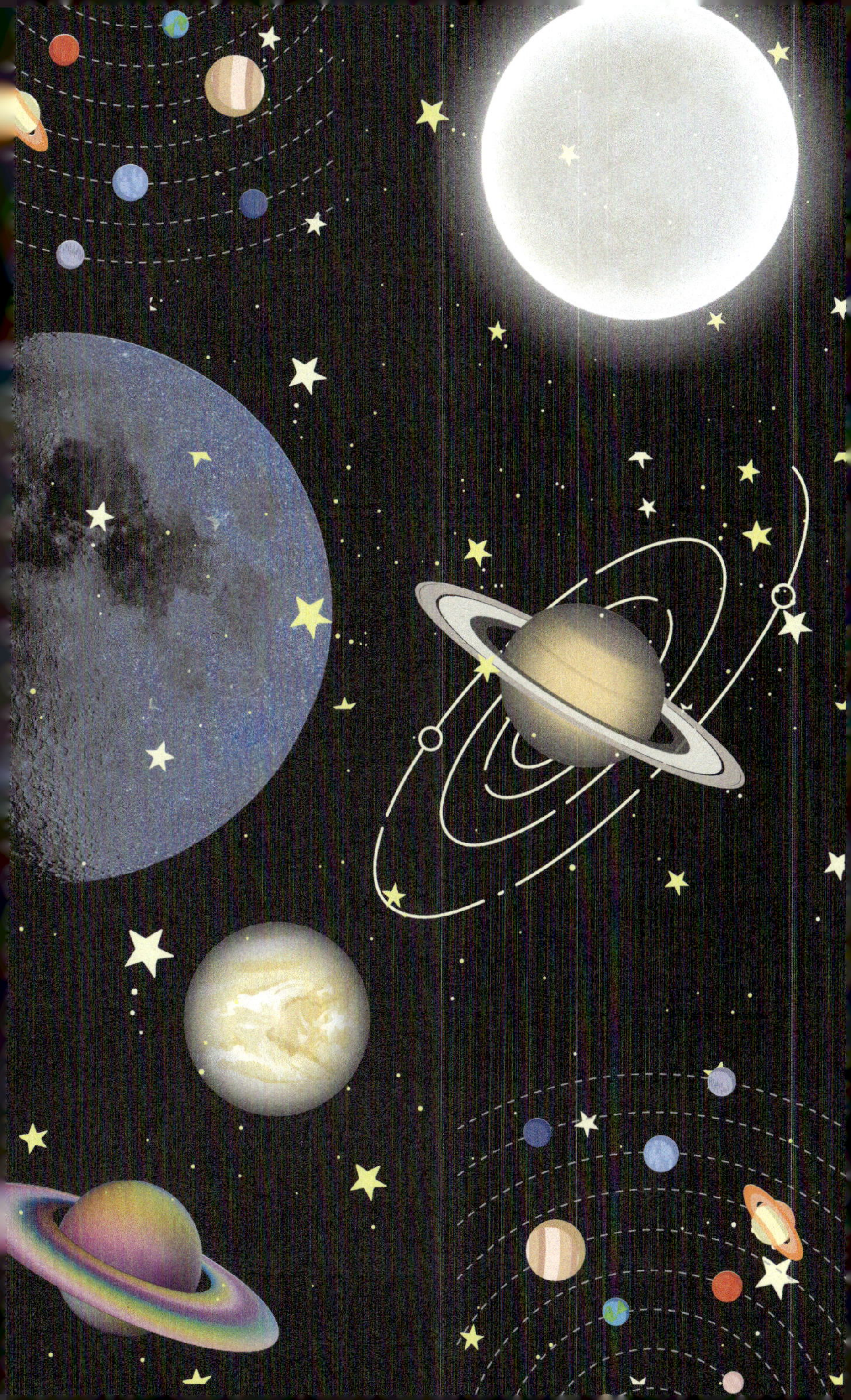

"When we focus on our gratitude, the tide of disappointment goes out and the tide of love rushes in."

KRISTIN ARMSTRONG

Ever heard of 'You attract what you are'?

In an article written by Sarah Kristenson, she explains that negativity results in negative results. If you set your mind for failure, you will fail. Conversely, people who radiate positivity tend to attract people with the same level of energy and drive. Like attracts like. So there is no way negative energy can attract positivity. If you put it in your mind that you deserve less, you will always attract less. For instance, some people believe they deserve better pay at their jobs. But how many of them actually do something to prove they deserve it? Develop actionable strategies to make it happen. If you want to get what you deserve, start acting like you deserve it. Believe and act like you are destined for greatness and you will receive it.

It is a possibility that you are what you attract because you do not align your thoughts with your desires. If you want to change who you are, first identify what you attract in your life and then devise ways to make the necessary changes. Your life will not improve if you do not change how you perceive things, your environment, and yourself. Cultivate positive feelings, emotions, and thoughts, aligning them with your desires. Irrespective of the challenges you might face in li fe, never let anything or anyone come between your goals. Whenever you feel like you are losing and you wish to quit, remember that change is sometimes inevitable to get what you want from life. Focus on the life you always imagined, visualise your dreams, and do not give up. If you truly want a better life, it doesn't happen by chance but by change. Studies carried out by scientists show that the more positive energy given towards something, the better it performs. The energy we put out always comes back to us. As our gratitude practice becomes more sensitive by focusing on what is good in our lives along with all of the blessings surrounding us, a certain magic begins to take hold.

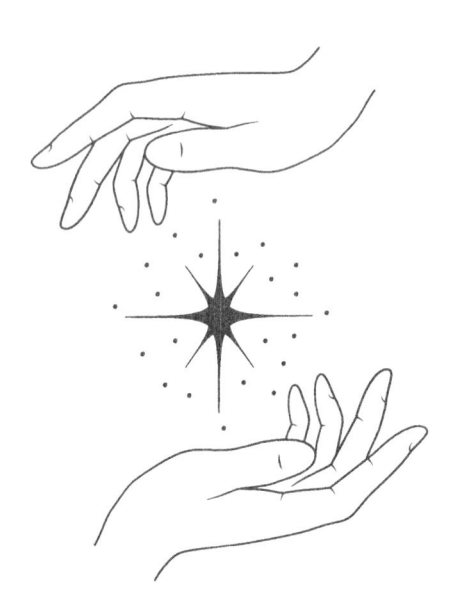

It's as if we send a message out to the universe to say "more of this please", which then causes the positive experiences in our life to flourish and grow.

"Gratitude will shift you to a higher frequency, and you will attract much better things."

Rhonda Byrne

Through the struggle, beauty is born

An experience that forced me to grow is when

I am grateful for this experience because

write down 3 ways you think this experience improved you as a person

What if I don't really feel that grateful for these things?

People who are new to the gratitude practice and are feeling some uncertainty about whether it's for them or not. I think when this question arises it's often evidence of some mind games and inner resistance at work, and a way that the ego behaves to try and talk us out of making some positive, empowered changes in our lives. On your good days and your bad days use simple thank yous to reinforce that positive state of mind such as saying "Today I'm grateful that I'm alive", or "Today I'm grateful that I have a roof over my head and food in my fridge when so many in the world are going without".

The intention with gratitude is not to put pressure on yourself to positive-think your way out of painful experiences or to deny their existence. Nor is it to create long lists that don't have any meaning to you and feel false or insincere. The aim is simply to direct your focus away from what's not going well in life, whilst still acknowledging the existence of the pain.

Cultivating an attitude of appreciation for the blessings life has to offer, no matter how small they may be, brings you back to the present moment and allows more space to open up to all that there is to be grateful for

"The more you practice gratitude, the more you see how much there is to be grateful for, and your life becomes an ongoing celebration of joy and happiness"

Don Miguel Ruiz

Today is _____

              and I am grateful for having

Every individual on earth is singularly unique.

No one is you and that is your power.

In the next few pages, I will ask you to write down all the things about your personality that you are grateful for

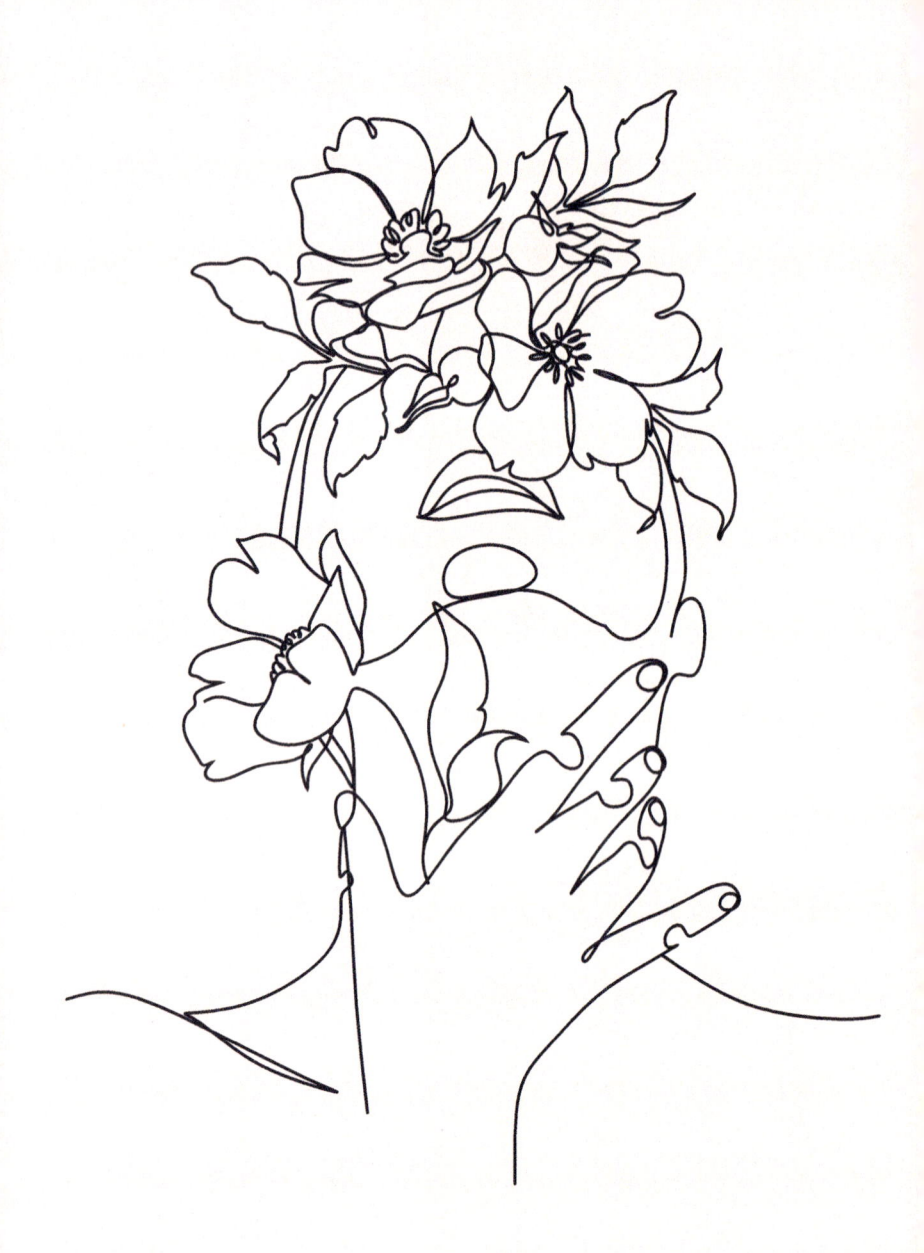

All the things about my personality that I am grateful for are

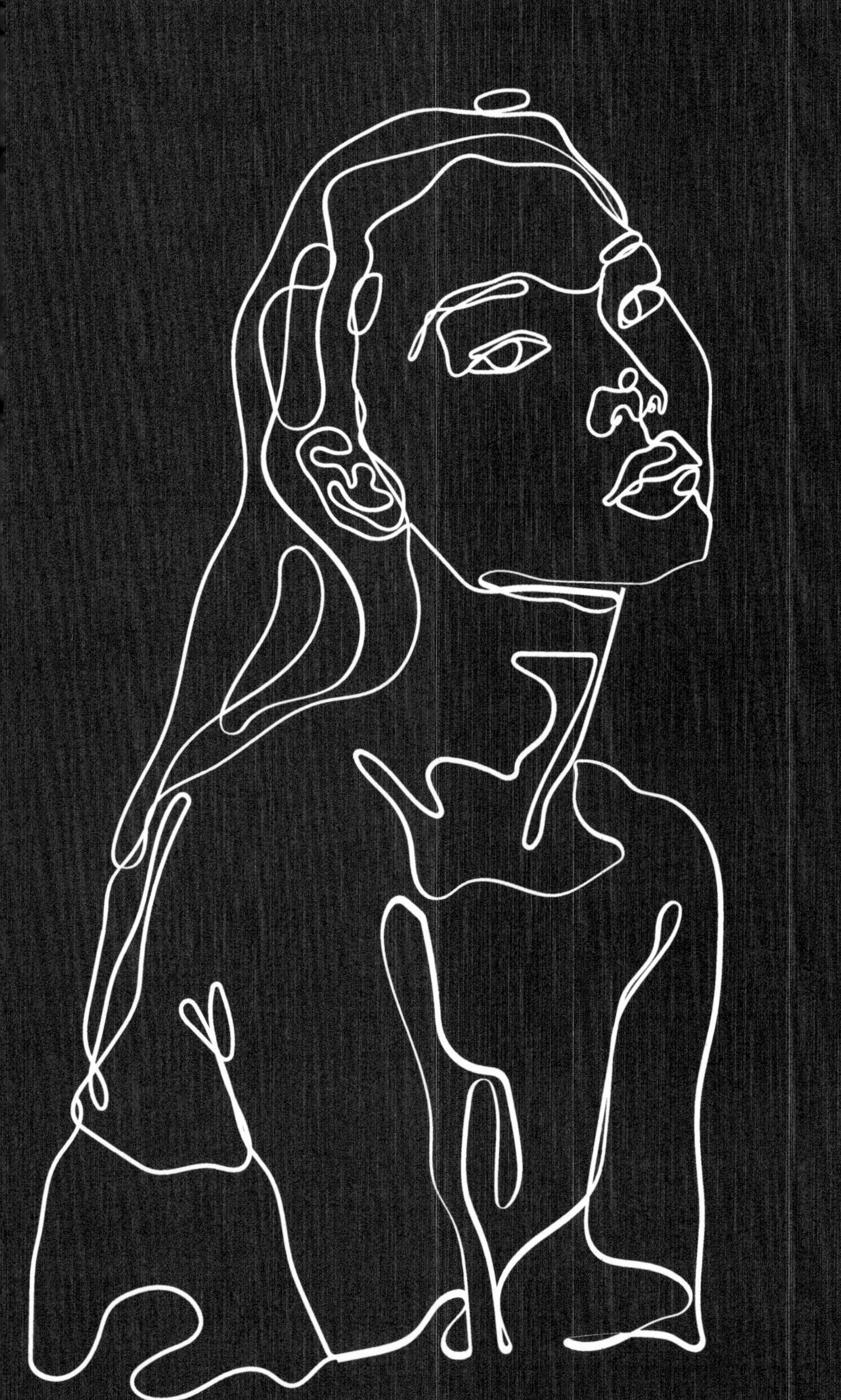

All the things about my personality that I would like to learn to be grateful for are

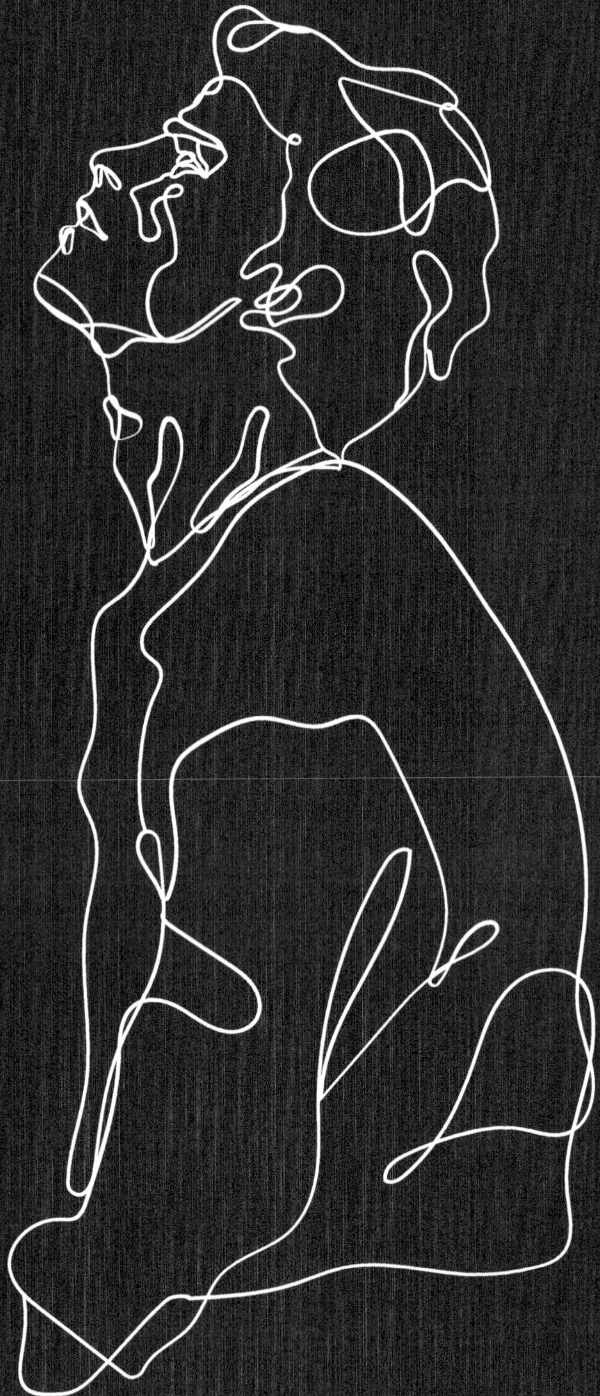

I am proud of myself because I am

1. ....
2. ....
3. ....

3 things today that went well

1. ....
2. ....
3. ....

Draw something that you are grateful for

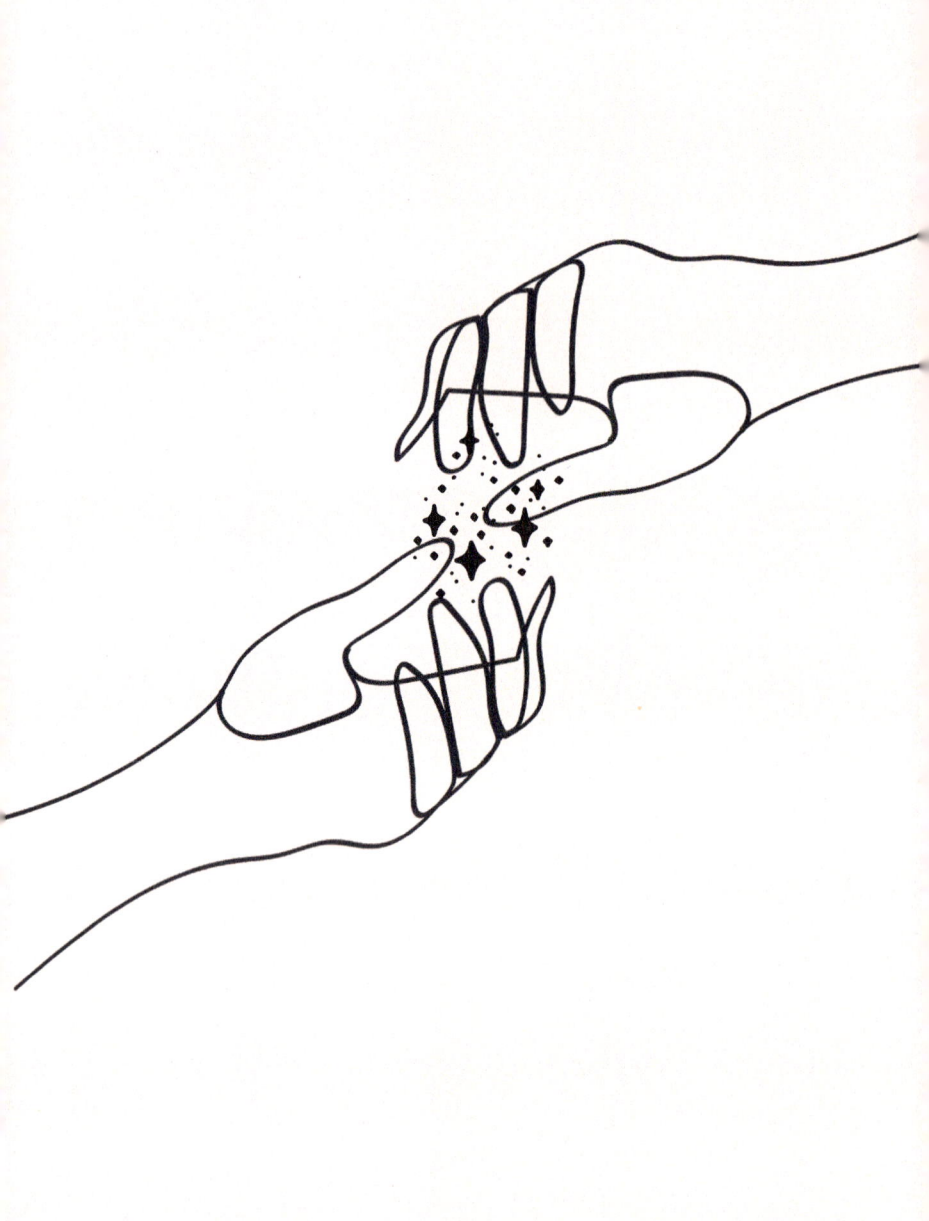

In this next section of the book, we will discuss relationships. This can be romantic relationships, friendships, relatives, colleagues, and so on.

As noted at the beginning of the book you may not be ready to speak about certain relationships and that is more than ok. Take your time, write what you feel, or simply come back to it when you please. We are going at your pace.

"Let us be grateful to the people who make us happy; they are the charming gardeners who make our souls blossom."

MARCEL PROUST

Think of a relationship you have had in your life and write down the things that you are grateful for that came from that relationship

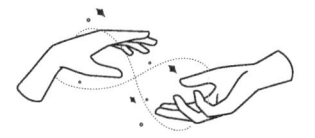

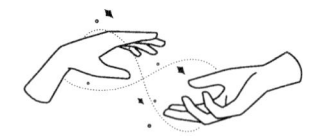

The Effects of writing down gratitude

American lawyer, television host, author, and motivational speaker Mel Robbins has expressed the intense positive impact that writing down one positive thing that happened throughout your day before you go to bed has on your life. Things as little as the fact that you got up on time, or perhaps there was no traffic that morning, maybe that you didn't argue with your kids or your parents, whatever it may be little or not, she makes it an important rule not to dismiss these things as they are in fact the things that are good and important.

If you'd prefer to do it in the morning as opposed to the night then that works equally as well too. This practice trains you to start to spot the good and fundamentally trains your brain to start focusing on the good, and by the law of attraction the more you focus on the good, the more good you will receive. It goes hand in hand.

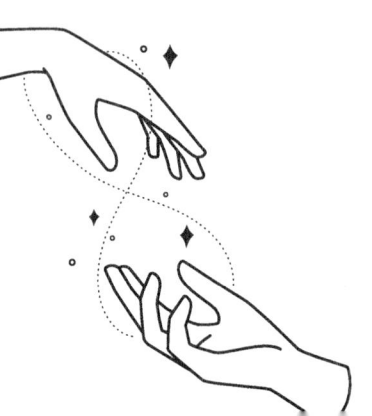

*So on that note,
today I am grateful for*

"If the only prayer you said was thank you, that would be enough."

MEISTER ECKHART

Your body is your temple. With you from the moment you are born on earth, up until the last moment you leave it.

In the next few pages I will prompt you to write about all the things about your body that you are grateful for. Write as much or as little as you desire. It is entirley up to you.

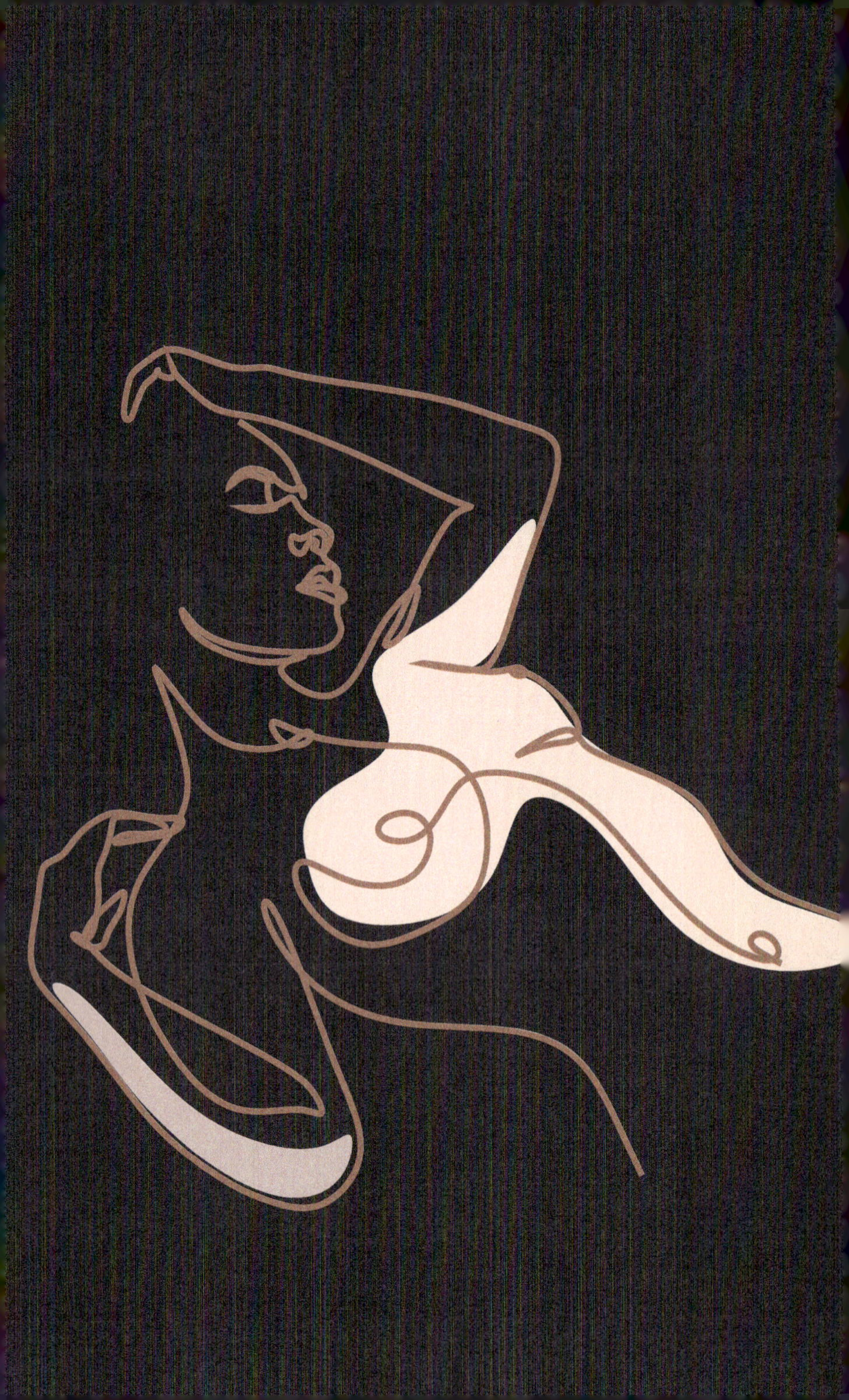

All the things about my body that I am grateful for are

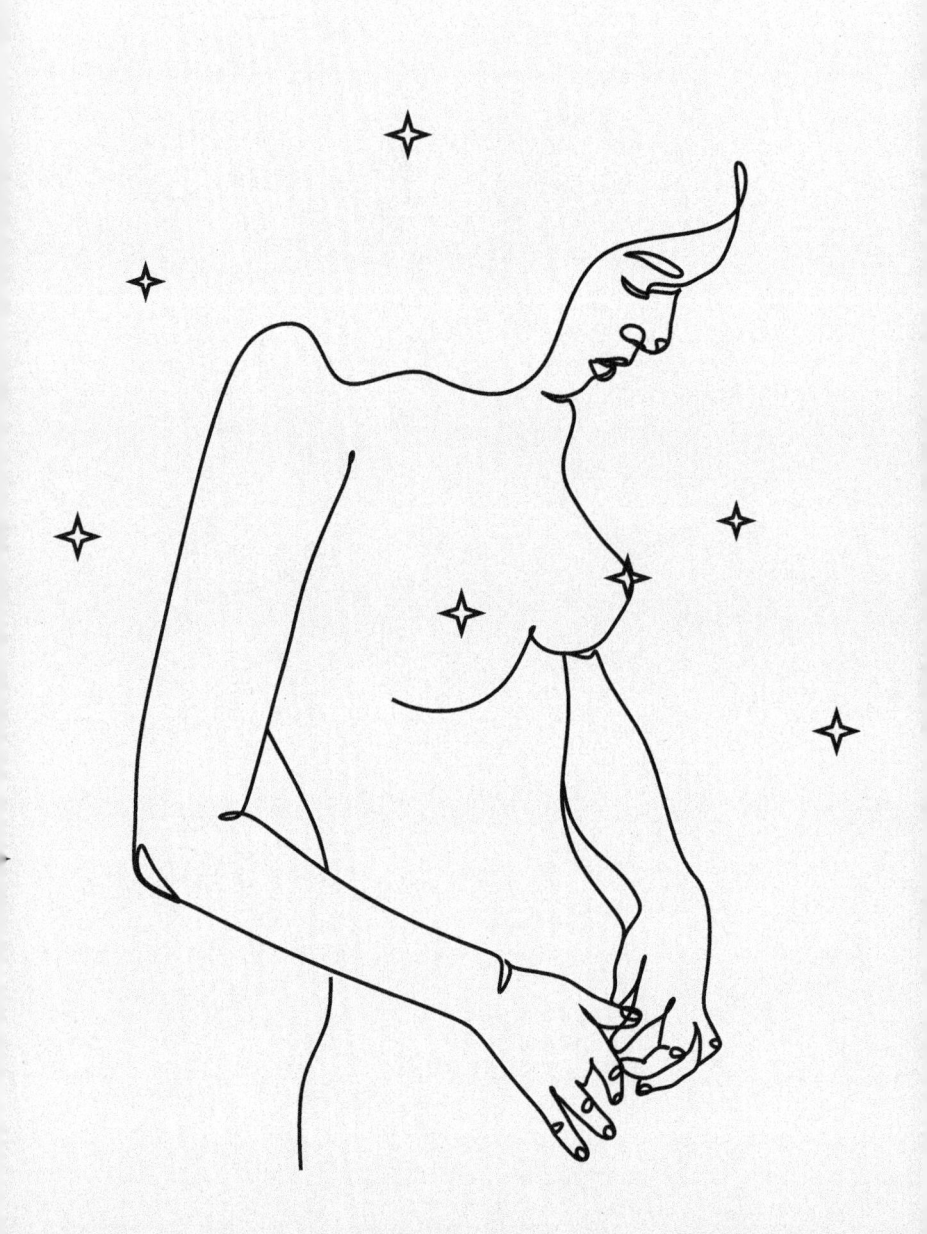

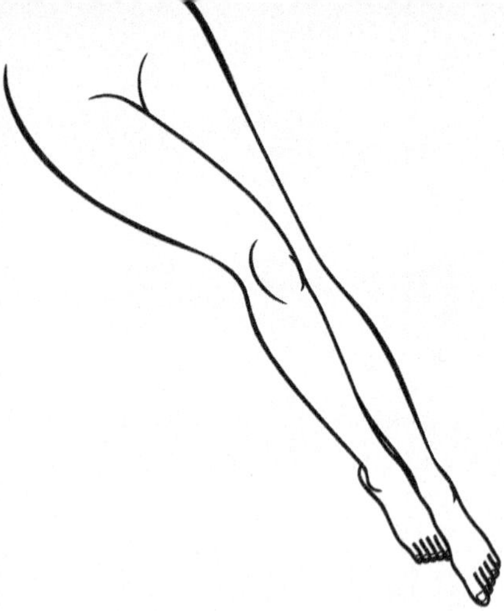
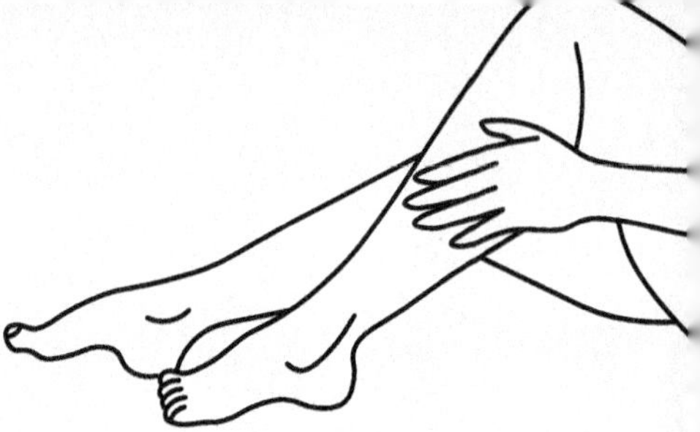
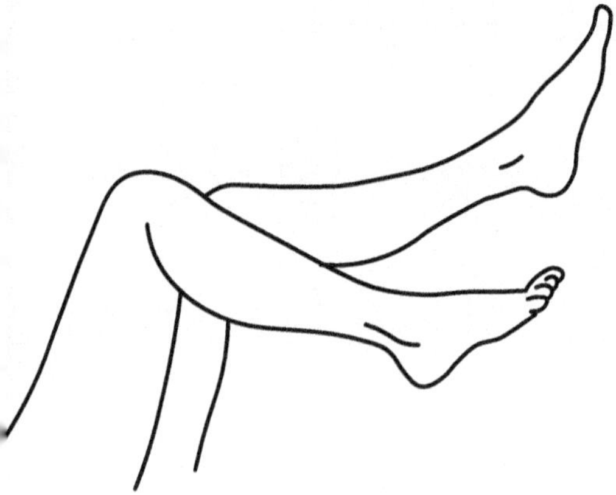
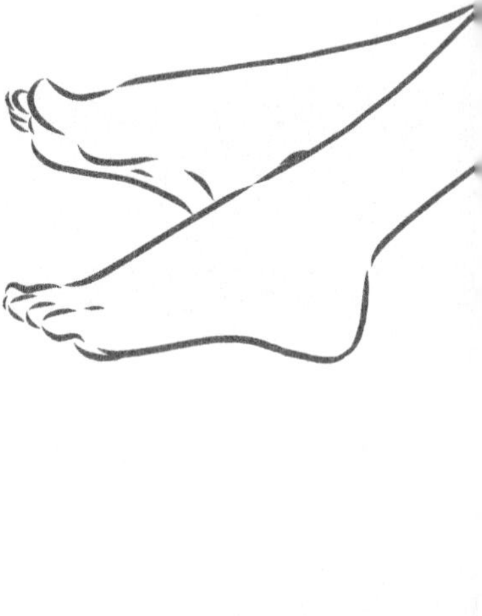
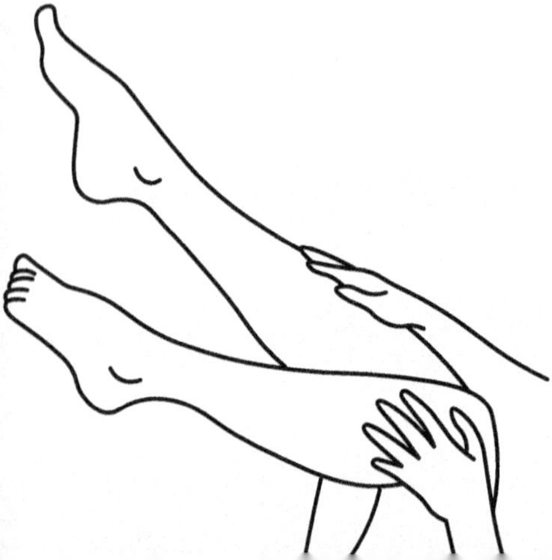
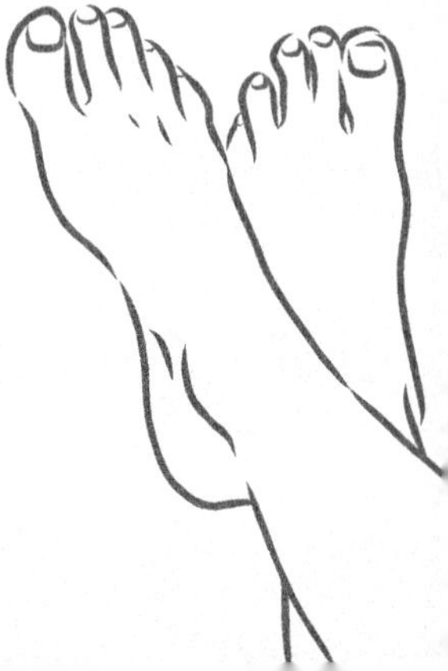

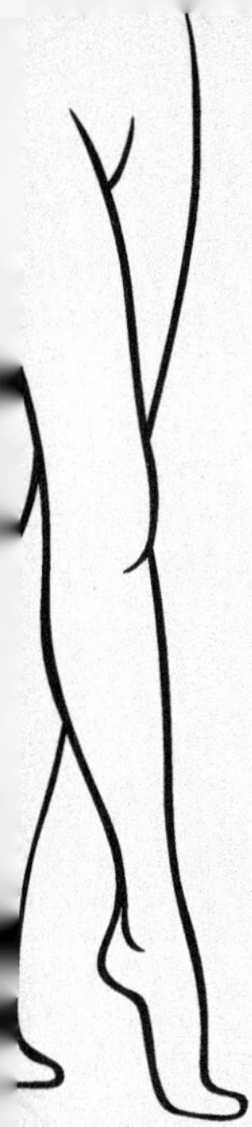
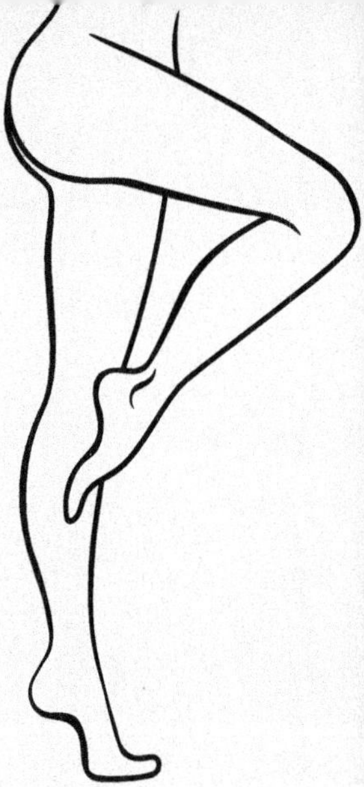
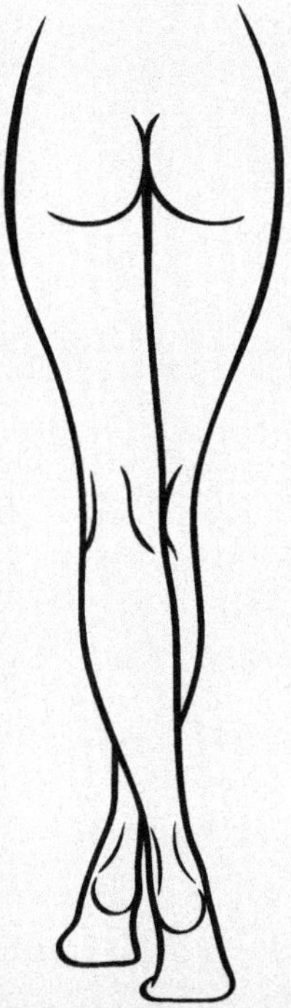
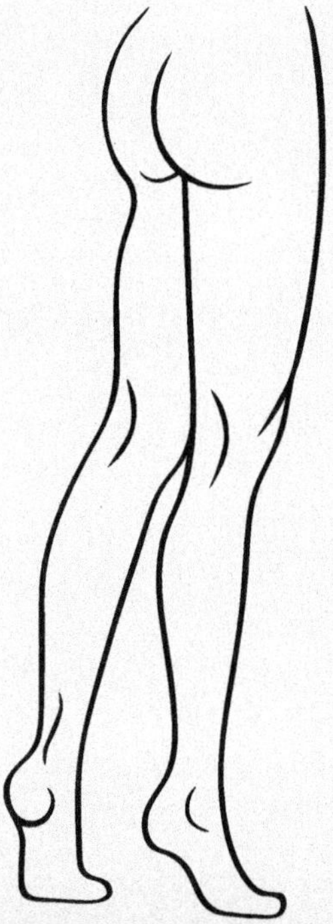

"Two kinds of gratitude: The sudden kind we feel for what we take; the larger kind we feel for what we give."

Edwin Arlington Robinson

In the next few pages, I will prompt you to write about all the things about your body that you aren't yet grateful for but would like to be. Again, write as much or as little as you desire, come back and add more, or don't. It is entirely up to you.

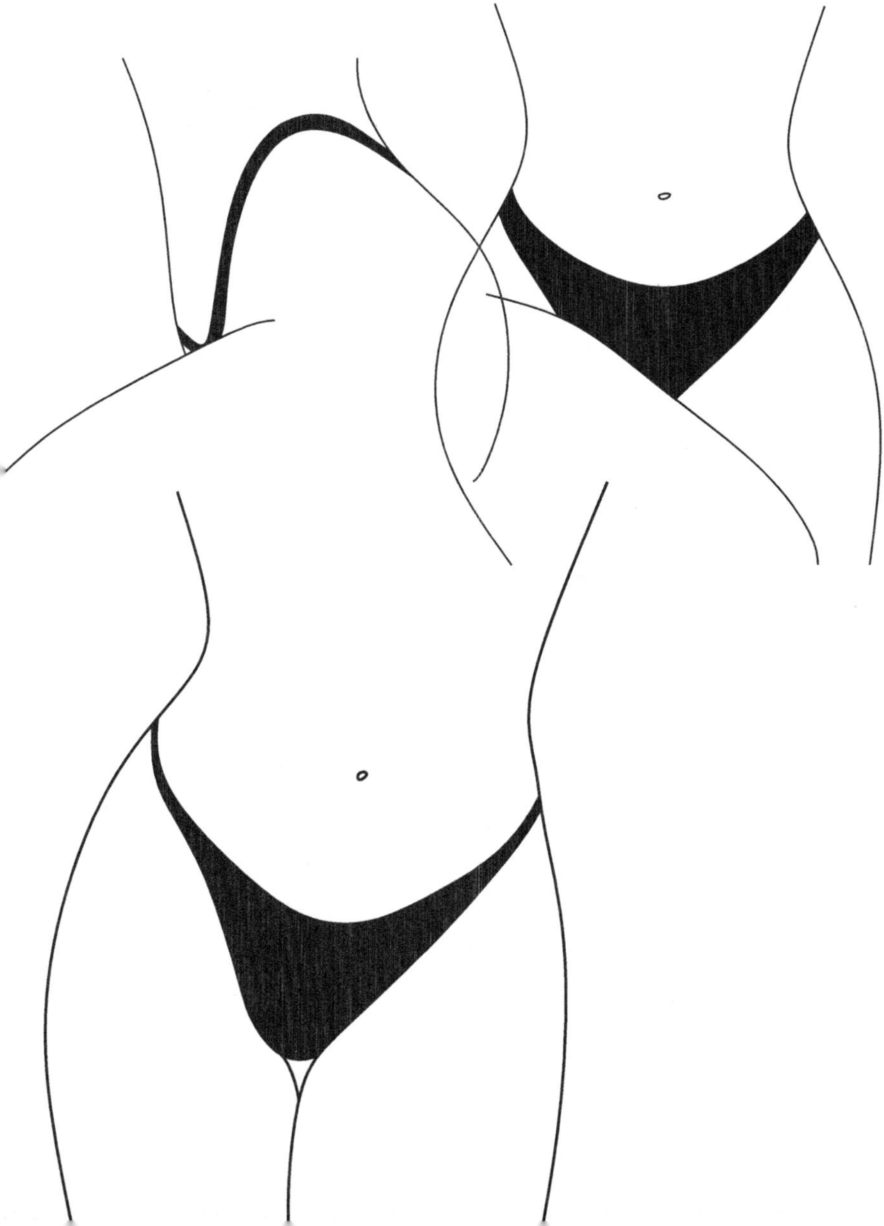

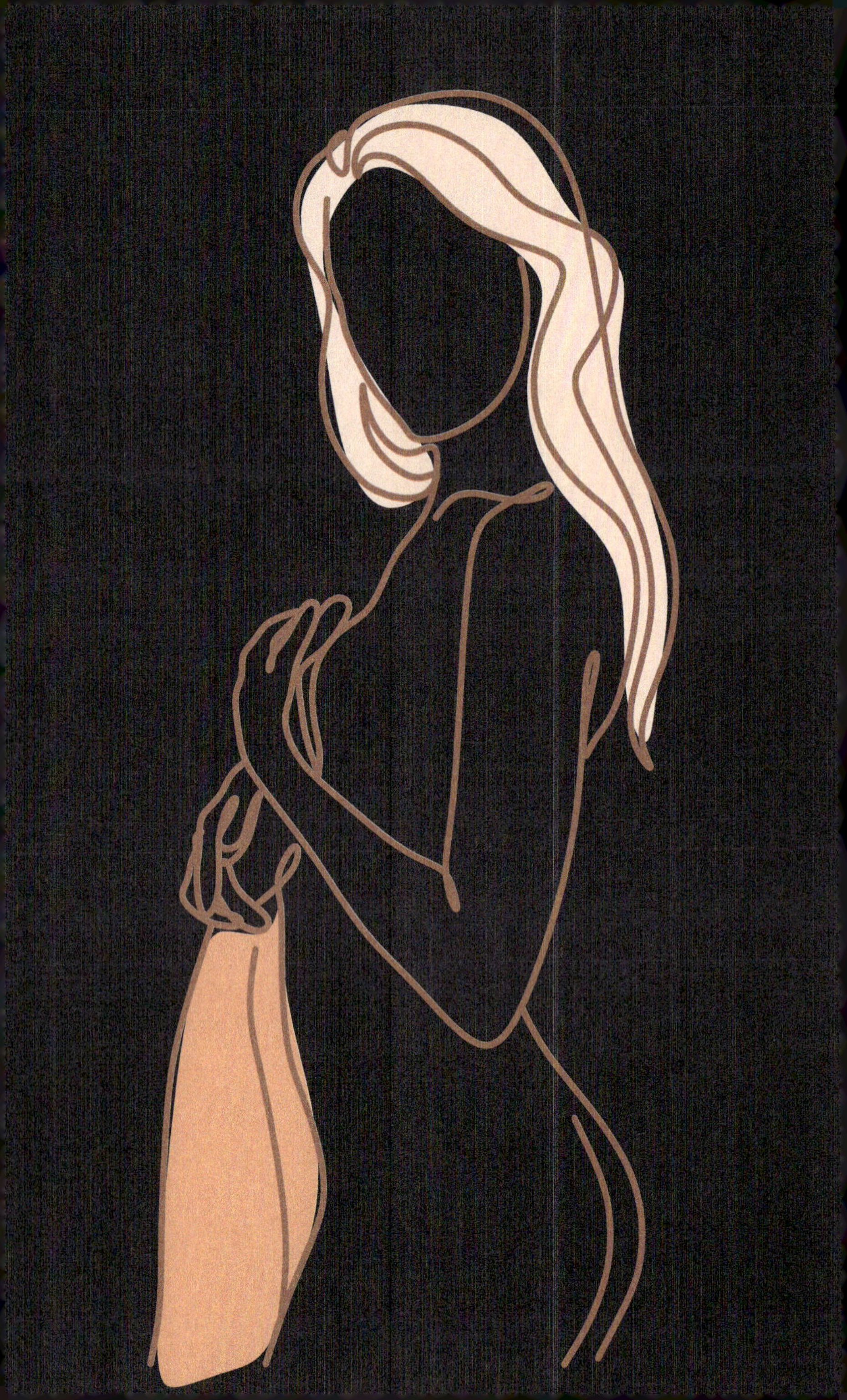

All the things about my body that I would like to learn to be grateful for are

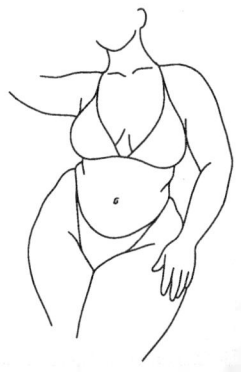

You were once here

And then here

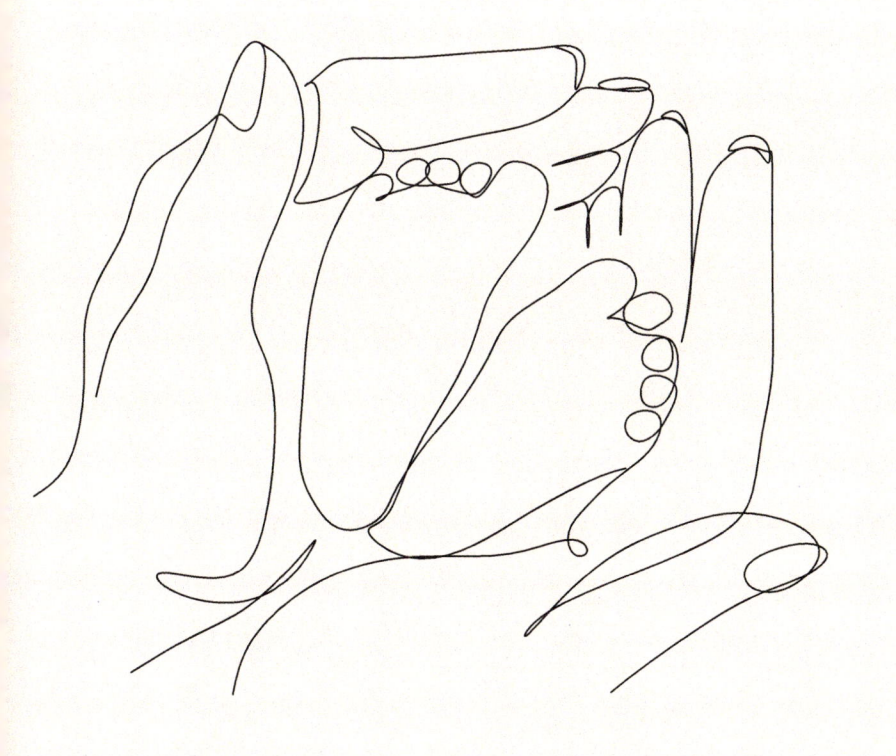

And now here

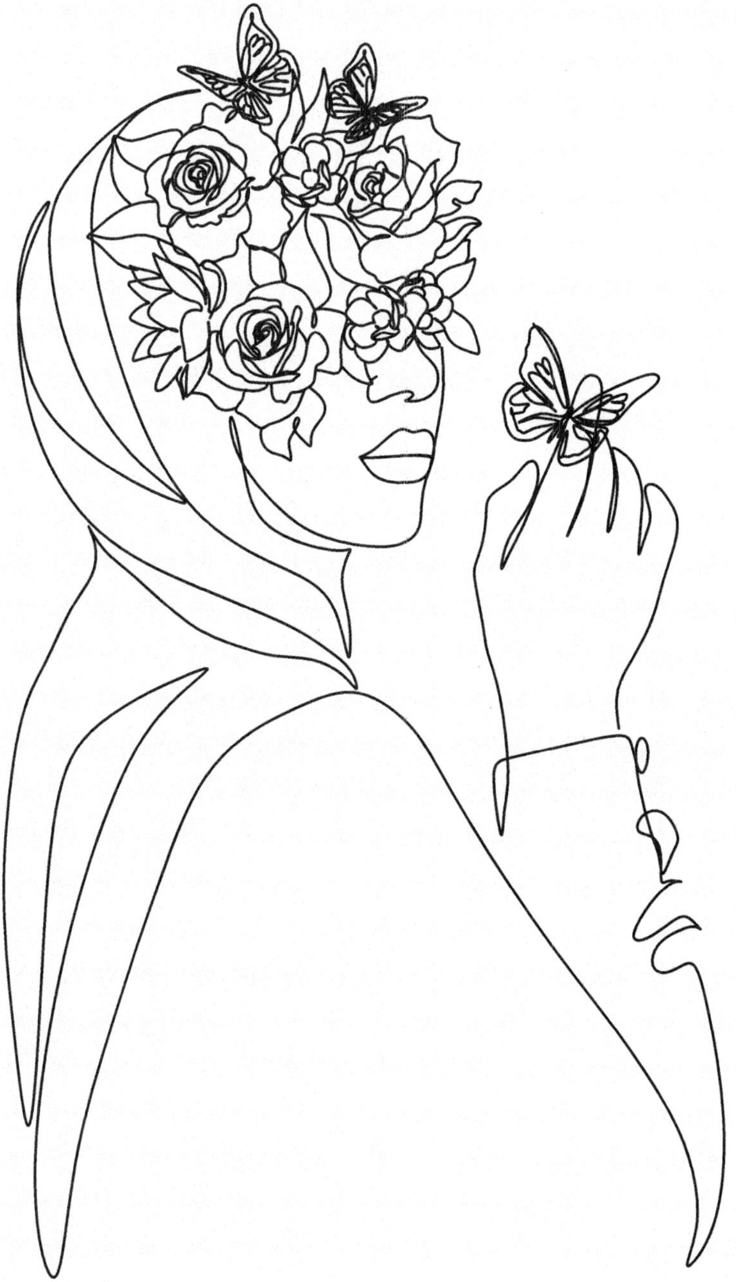

Write down some of the ways you show your body gratitude by taking care of it if there aren't any, write down ways you'd like to start

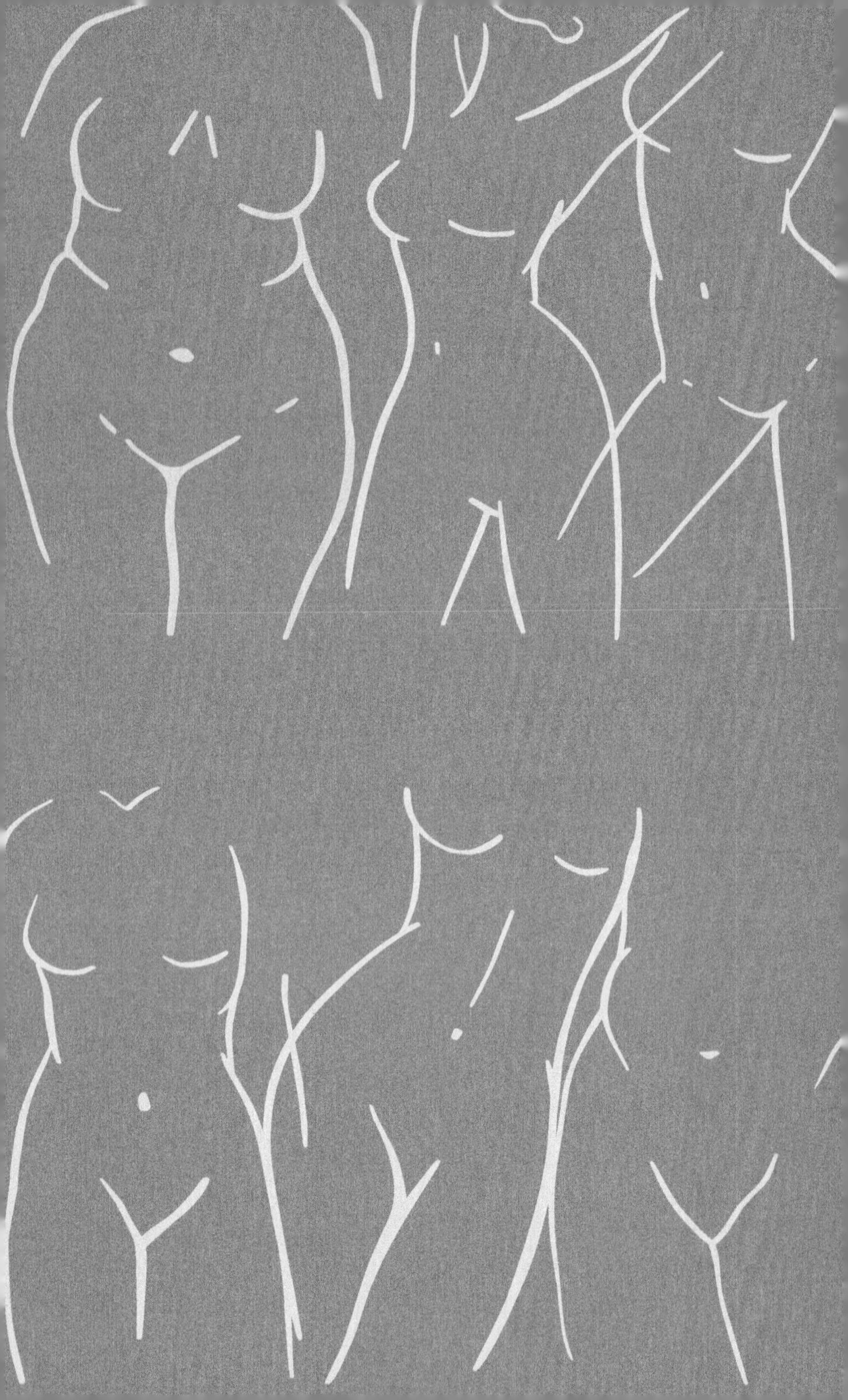

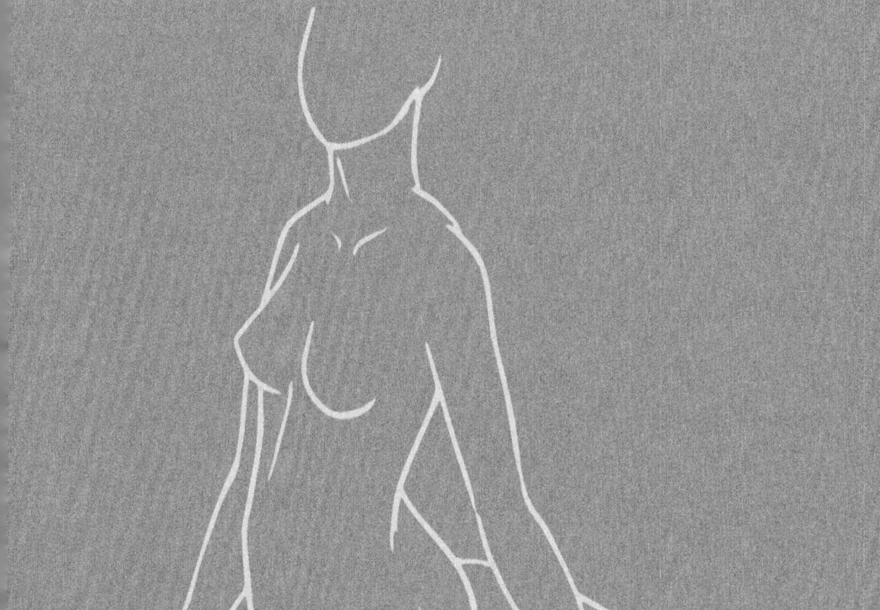

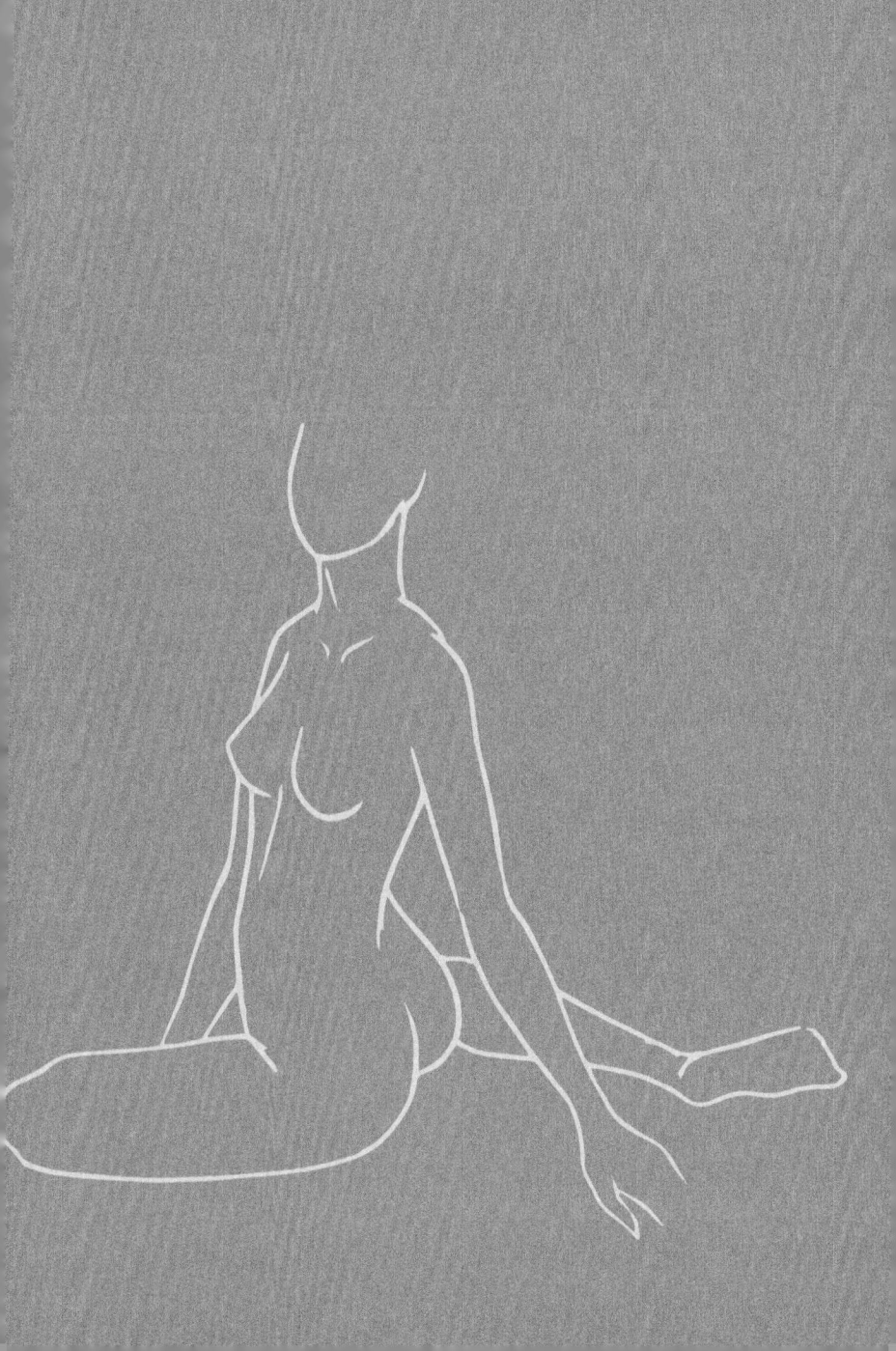

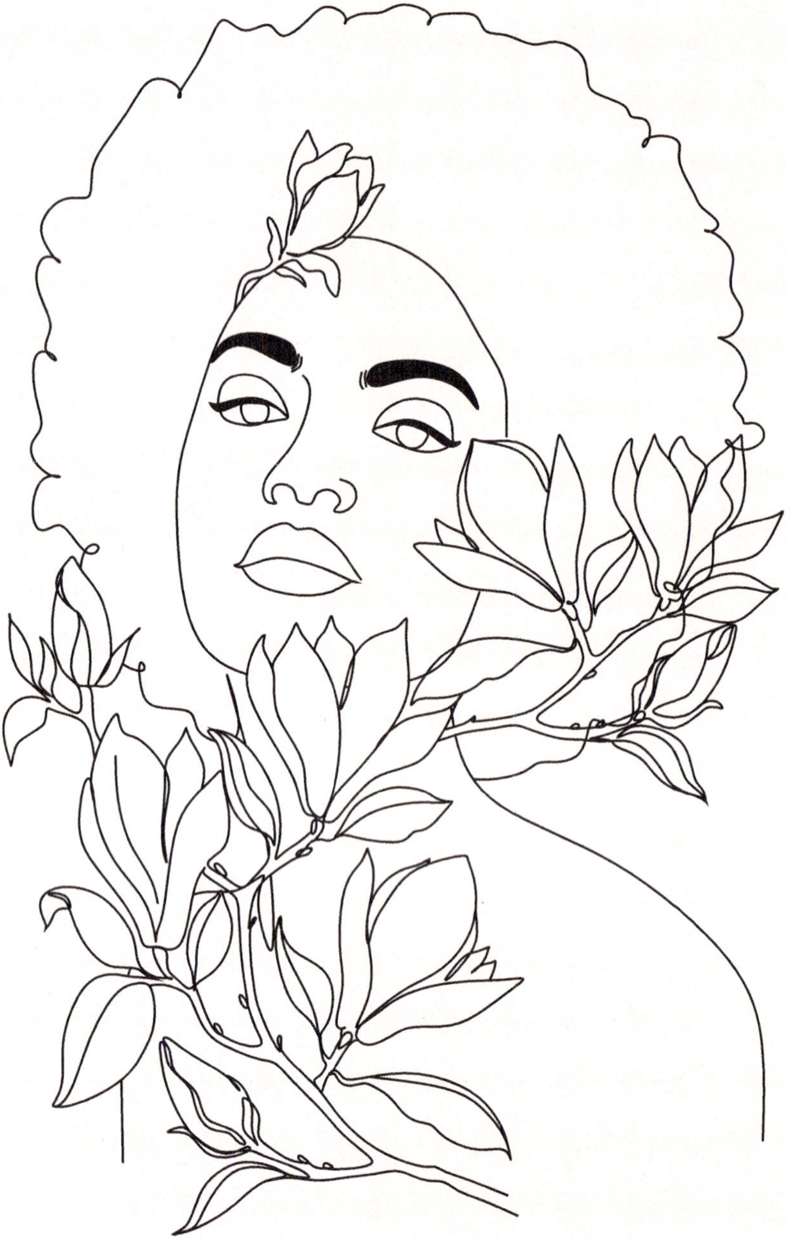

My favourite features about my hair are

My favourite features about my face are

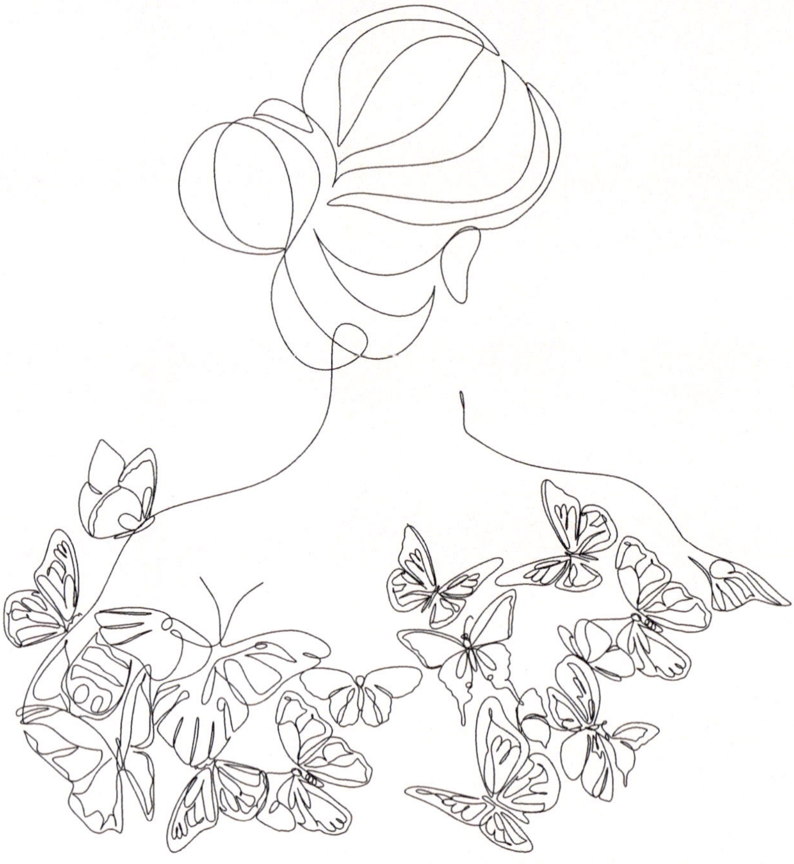

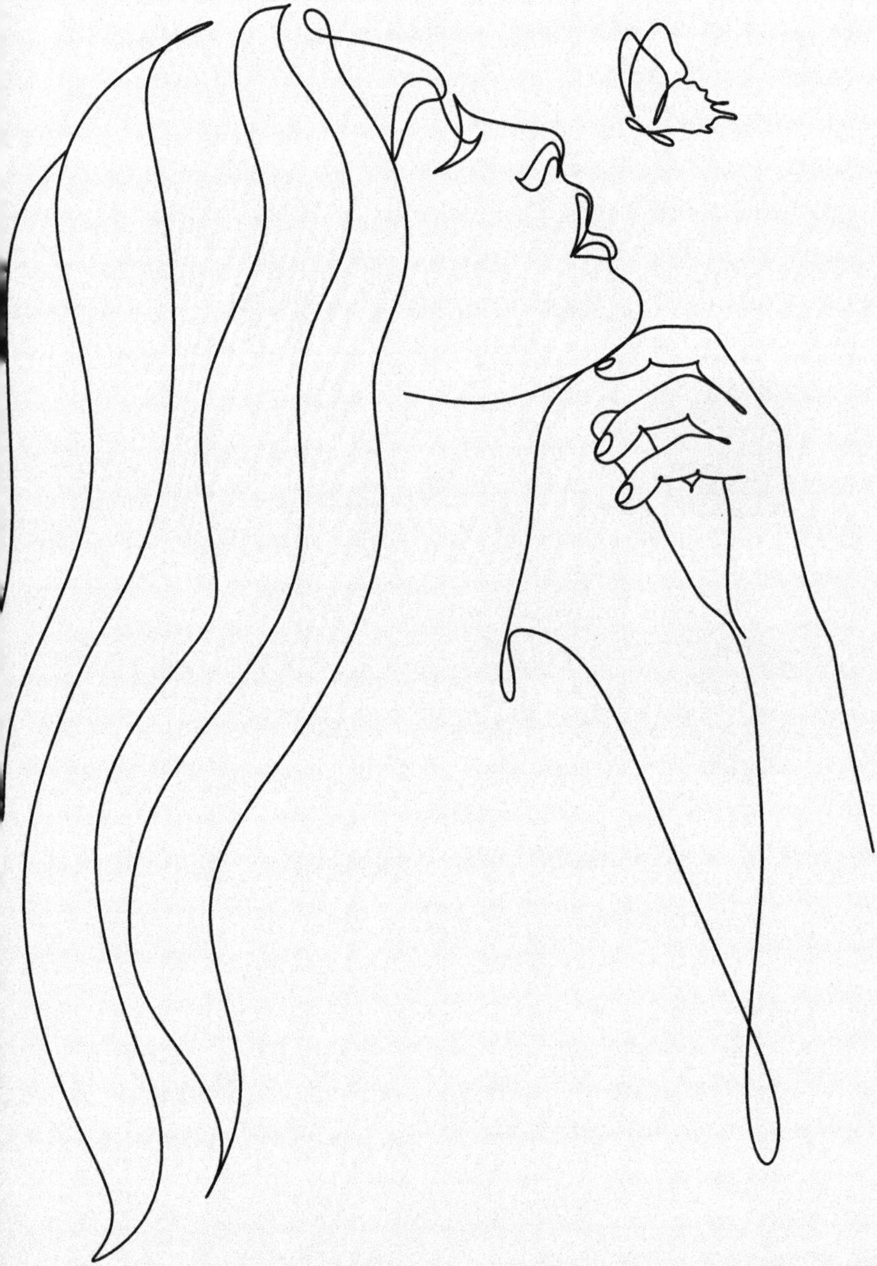

Do you appreciate those birthmarks that make you, those scars that shape you...

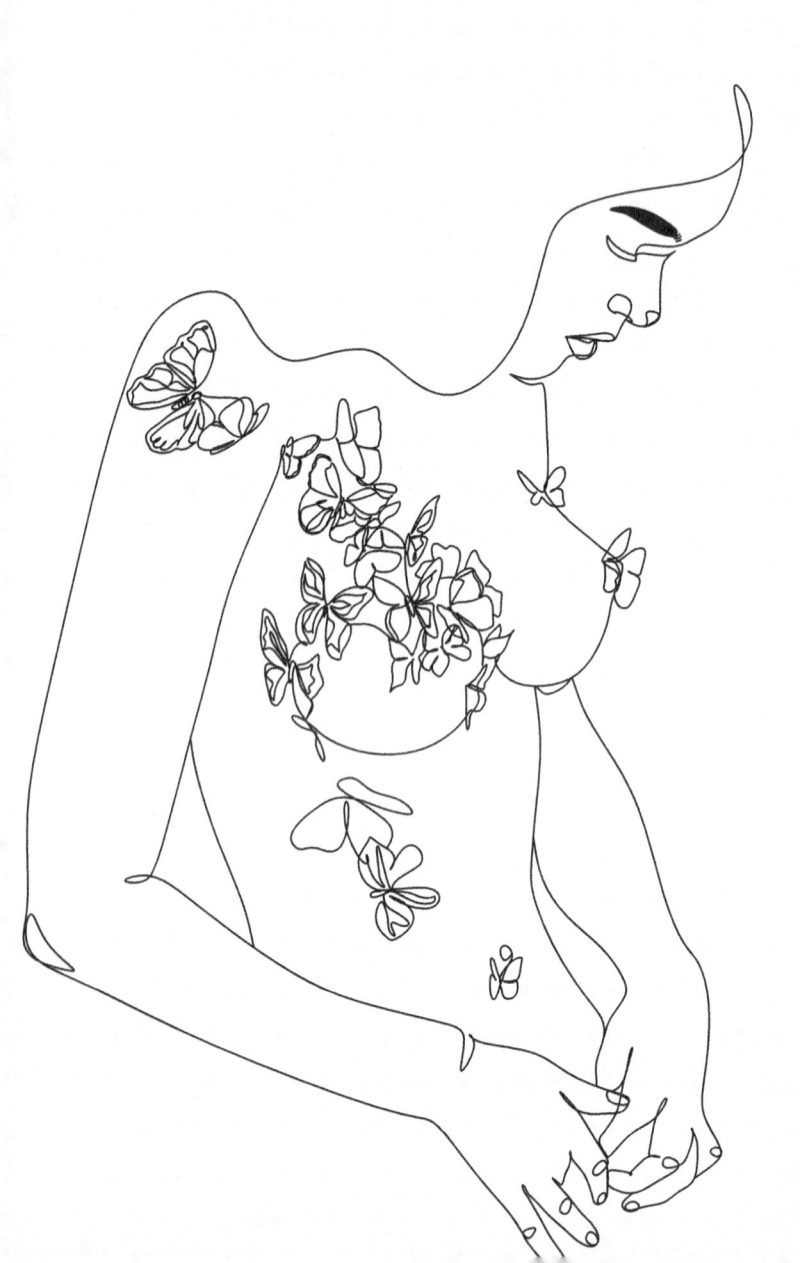

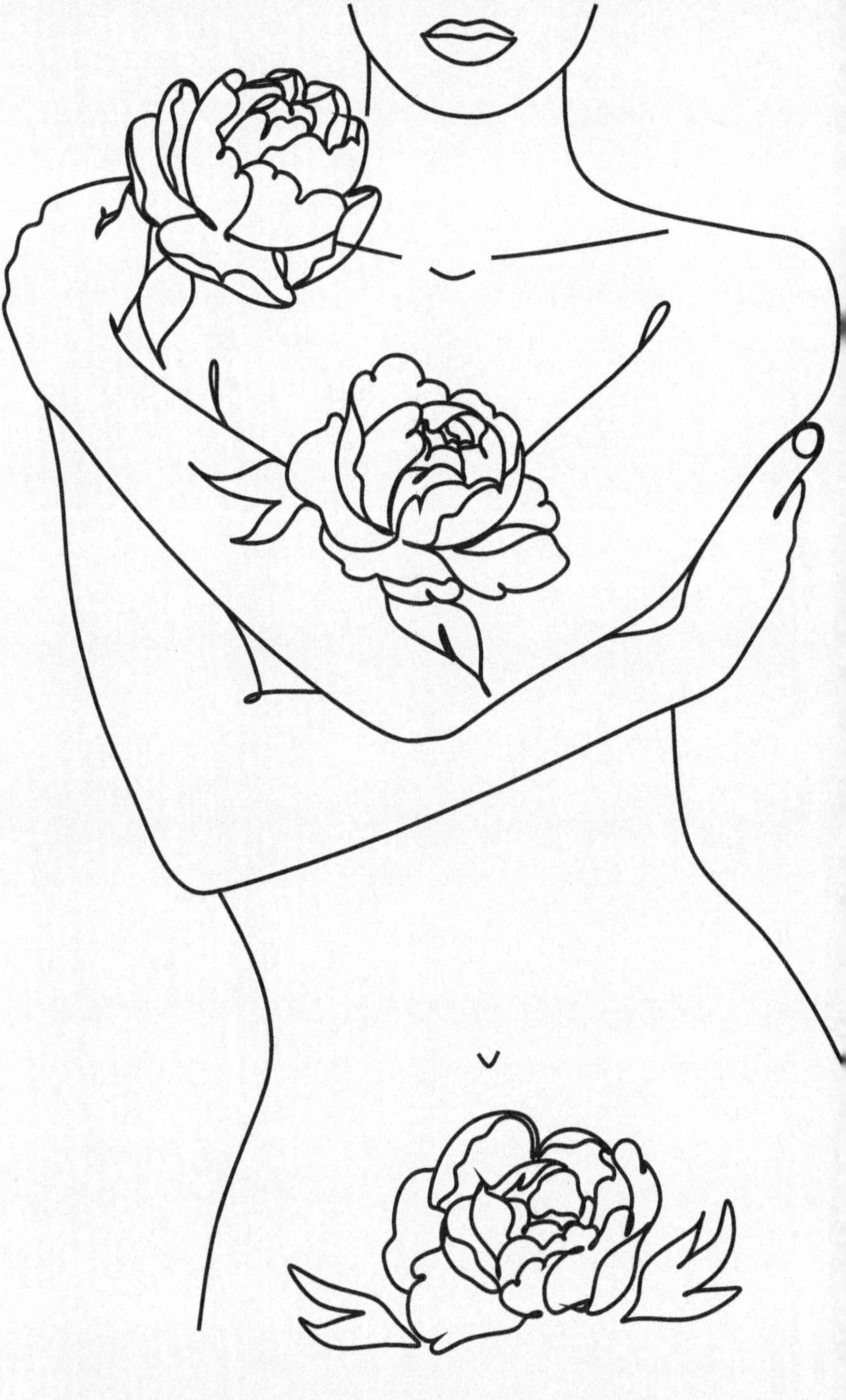

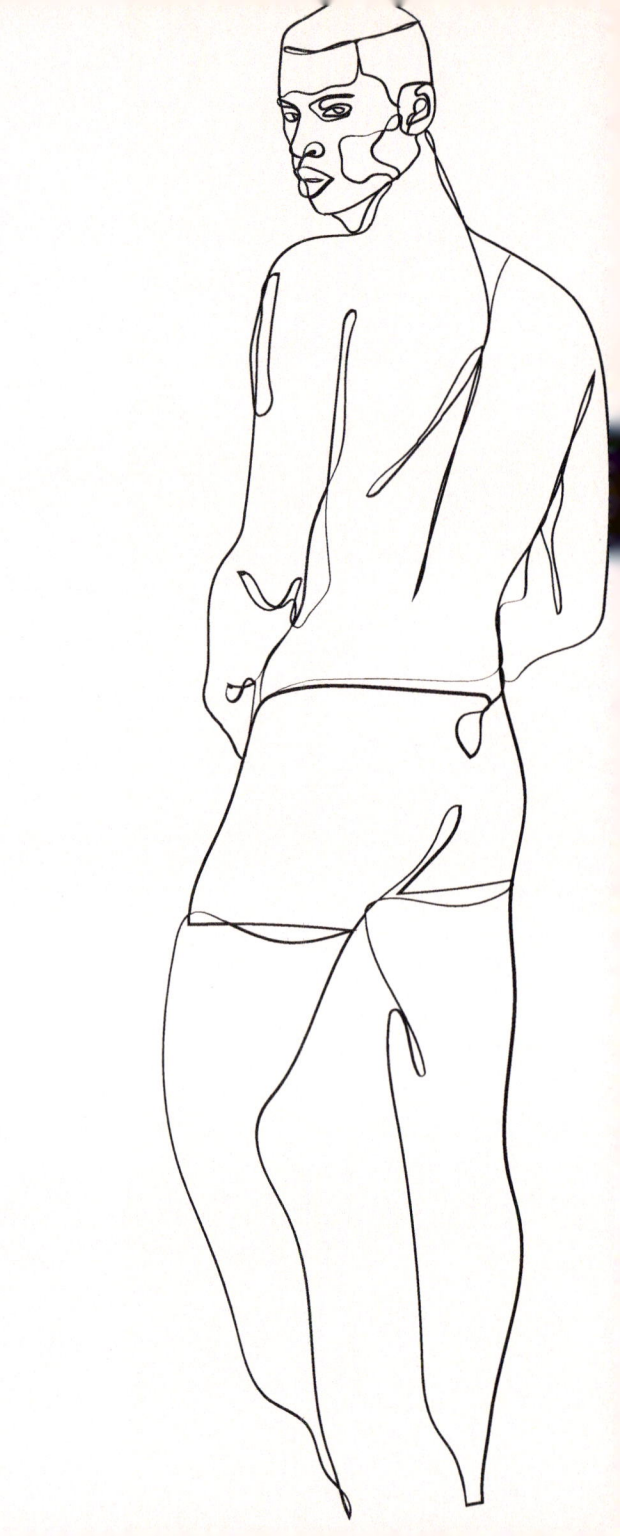

I know this book is based on the practice of gratitude however, I would like to mention the practice of visualisation as I believe it is an amazing tool not only to improve your gratitude levels but to improve the overall quality of your life. Mel Robbins puts it extremely well. Backed up by science, visualisation has proved to be an extraordinary powerful skill. She explains that our brains are gigantic detective machines and that they are constantly looking for evidence. So just a few minutes before bed and when you wake up, take 60 seconds to visualise whatever you want. Visualise yourself having a good day at work, visualise yourself understanding the topics your professor is explaining and the happiness you'll feel knowing that you're doing well.

What I found super compelling about visualisation is that our brains can't tell the difference between something that actually happened to us and the things that we imagine are happening to us. It's like you have a crappy day, and at the end of the day you visualise yourself having an amazing day, your brain won't even know your day has been crappy. It has a significant positive impact on the way you think and feel allowing you to be more open to the feeling of gratitude. Also, what studies have proven is that visualising yourself doing things, actually develops the skill and helps you to improve the skills just as if you were actually doing them. Which I believe is incredible. Commit to doing this and see the positive effect that this may have on your life.

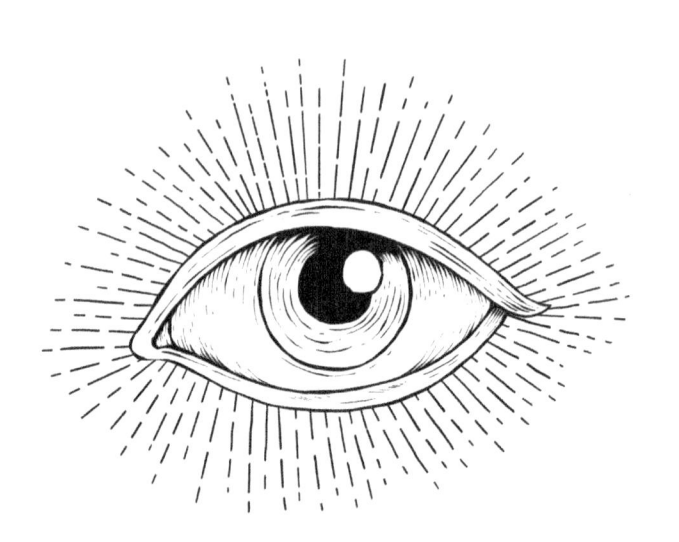

3 reasons that I am grateful for my home

1. ....
2. ....
3. ....

Significant asests in my life at present

1. ....
2. ....
3. ....

Draw something that you are grateful for

Living in the past

"I looked around and thought about my life. I felt grateful. I noticed every detail. That is the key to time travel. You can only move if you are actually in the moment. You have to be where you are to get where you need to go."

Amy Poehler

Living in a constant state of what was never allows you to experience the present moment as you should. Conflicted about what went wrong how things could have been different, each dwelling moment has a bigger impact on you than you may realise. Past events that you can't seem to escape leave you trapped in a state of sorrow focused on what was and never what is.

To leave the past in the past and start living in the present, sometimes, just the thing you need is to talk about it with someone other than yourself, someone you feel comfortable with, or perhaps a stranger, such as therapy. Lay it all out. Be honest with yourself about how you feel and why you think it is still affecting you until this day. By starting that conversation you become more and more comfortable speaking about it over time and once you're comfortable with it, you can heal from it. It may take some time for you to be at peace with, but you can figure out what steps you need to take to create a safer environment around that subject in hopes of moving on.

Living in fear of being hurt again will only hurt you 10x more, as you stop yourself from experiencing all of the things that you should be

"Gratitude makes sense of our past, brings peace for today, and creates a vision for tomorrow."

Melody Beattie

Living in the future

The future is unknown. You can plan and plan and plan, and have an entirely different outcome to which you heavily relied on to finally be 'happy'. By all means, setting goals for yourself and the required steps on how you will achieve them is one of the best things you can do. On the other hand, not being able to enjoy the journey (which is the most important part btw) will essentially ruin the way in which you experience everything.

By neglecting your appreciation for the journey, you miss out on enjoying all that life has to offer not just the achievements. For it is the journey that will make you more resilient, more knowledgeable, and essentially the person you will become. Learn to enjoy the steps you take for if you don't, true happiness will forever be unattainable.

Find a way to step out of the mindset of 'I'll finally be happy when I earn x amount, have the car of my dreams, and live in a beautiful apartment with a city view'. Once acquired, you'll find yourself in a state of confusion. Not sure why you don't feel all the things you expected to, an ***anti-climax.*** You'll be convincing yourself that you just need a few more things that you don't have, to feel this happy and complete feeling that you so desperately crave. The truth is that you can acquire all you have ever dreamed of and more, but if y ou are not grateful for what you have now, what makes you think that you will be grateful for all you will have in the future.

"Be thankful for what you have; you'll end up having more. If you concentrate on what you don't have, you will never, ever have enough."

Oprah Winfrey

Some days we will struggle to feel grateful and that's okay

No one can feel constant gratitude at all times it's simply not human. so I would like to kindly remind you that there are going to be days, weeks, months, or even years when nothing feels as though it is going right and as if all odds are working against you instead of with you. But in most cases, all it takes is a shift of your focus from the bad to the good. Watch what happens when you concentrate on the good and stop giving your undivided attention and energy to the bad. When you keep working a muscle it grows stronger over time, the same applies to when you focus on the good that you will receive more of it over time.

"This is a wonderful day I have never seen this one before."

MAYA ANGELOU

Did you go out today or stay home?

Tick the elements that you enjoyed the most

Stayed home   Went out

○ **The time I spent alone/with others**   **The people I met** ○

○ **The work I got done**   **The places I visited** ○

○ **The comfort I felt**   **The day I had** ○

○ **The movies/shows I watched**   **The fresh air** ○

Today is _____

and I am grateful for having

I am grateful to have these things in my life because they make me feel

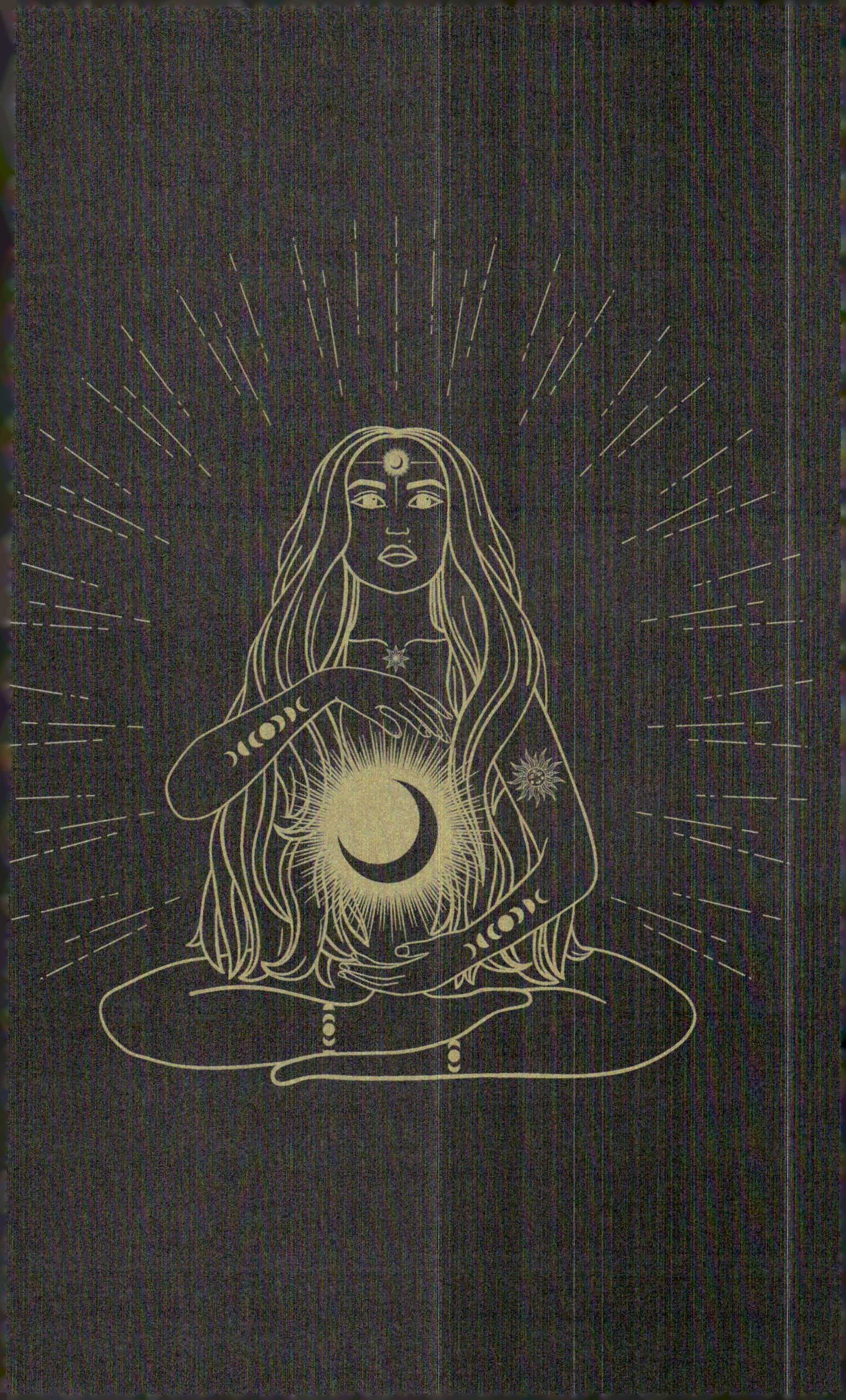

Struggling to feel grateful?

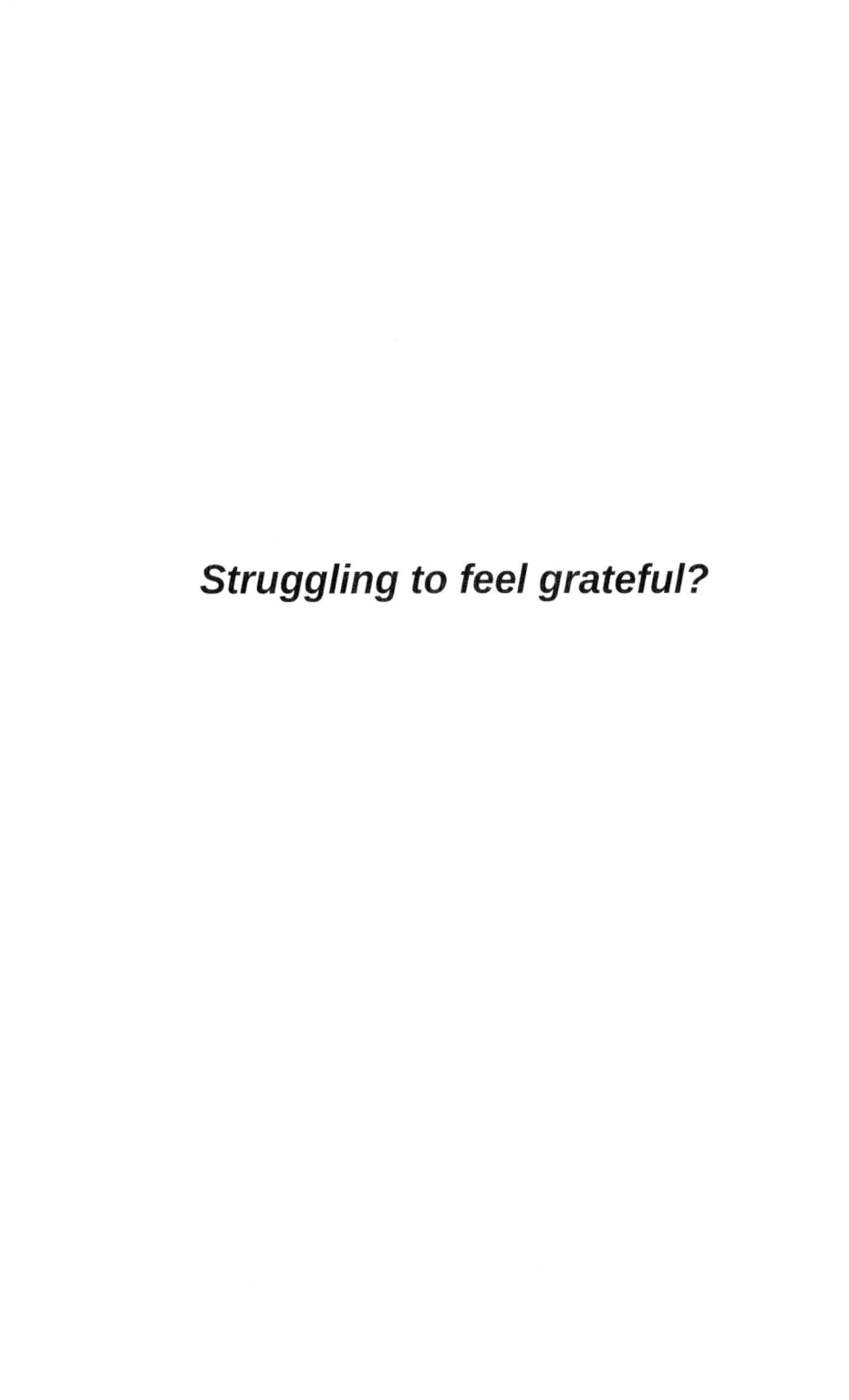

Here are some ways to help you cultivate gratitude

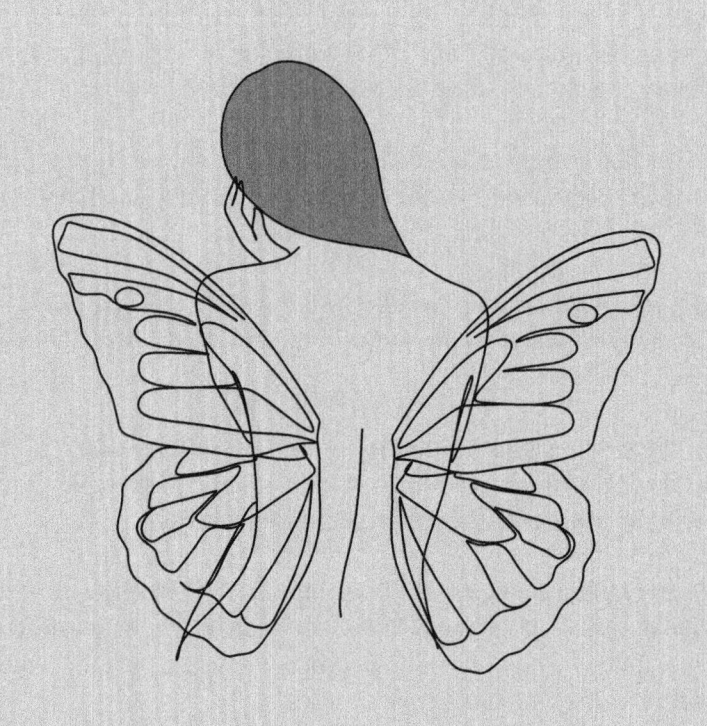

Written In Harvard Health Publishing here are some ways you can help overcome your gratitude struggles:

1. Write a thank-you note. You can make yourself happier and nurture your relationship with another person by writing a thank-you letter or email expressing your enjoyment and appreciation of that person's impact on your life.

Send it, or better yet, deliver and read it in person if possible. Make a habit of sending at least one gratitude letter a month. Once in a while, write one to yourself.

2. Thank someone mentally. No time to write? It may help just to think about someone who has done something nice for you, and mentally thank the individual.

3. Keep a gratitude journal. Make it a habit to write down or share with a loved one thoughts about the gifts you've received each day.

4. Count your blessings. Pick a time every week to sit down and write about your blessings reflecting on what went right or what you are grateful for each week.

5. Sometimes it helps to pick a number — such as three to five things — that you will identify each week. As you write, be specific and think about the sensations you felt when something good happened to you.

6. Pray. People who are religious can use prayer to cultivate gratitude.

7. Meditate. Mindfulness meditation involves focusing on the present moment without judgment.

Although people often focus on a word or phrase (such as "peace"), it is also possible to focus on what you're grateful for (the warmth of the sun, a pleasant sound, etc)

"The soul that gives thanks can find comfort in everything; the soul that complains can find comfort in nothing."

Hannah Whithall Smith

Wherever you go, I'll follow

If you currently have a partner write down all the things that you are grateful for about them

If not, write down all the things you would be grateful for in a partner

"At times, our own light goes out and is rekindled by a spark from another person. Each of us has cause to think with deep gratitude of those who have lighted the flame within us."

Albert Schweitzer

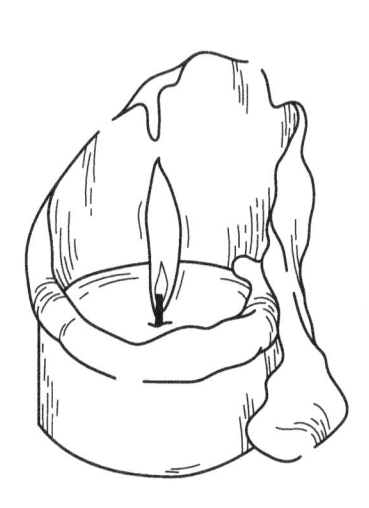

Think about the partners you have had in the past, write down all the things your are grateful for that came from having them as a partner

"If you fail to carry around with you a heart of gratitude for the love you've been so freely given, it is easy for you not to love others as you should."

PAUL DAVID TRIPP

Two approaches to expressing gratitude

Think of the memories that make you happy (I hope that there are a few you can recall). Now think of the things that allowed you to have that happy memory.

For example, maybe one of your happy memories is a day you spent out on a school trip with all of your friends, and on that trip, you visited an amazing museum, ate food you thoroughly enjoyed and shared wonderful laughs on a beautiful summers day. There are two ways in which I like to express my gratitude.

Starting with number one

1. *The Deeper Approach*

By using a deeper approach you look at the root of all the important factors that went into the possibility to have that experience. For example, you are grateful for your parents/providers for allowing you to go on this trip and having the jobs that provided them with the necessary means to pay for your trip and also the food and other luxuries you enjoyed on your trip. You could be grateful for the opportunity to make friends, as you live in a country that allows you to go to school and have an education, and thus the ability to make the friendships you now have. Lastly, you could be grateful to a higher power or whoever you believe keeps a watchful eye over you, who kept you safe whilst you attended the trip and allowed the weather to be good.

"Let us rise up and be thankful, for if we didn't learn a lot today, at least we learned a little, and if we didn't learn a little, at least we didn't get sick, and if we got sick, at least we didn't die; so, let us all be thankful."

Buddha

As someone who likes to analyse things, this might be your most preferred way to express your gratitude. However, if you are someone with a less analytical personality, option two may be a better fit.

2.The Simpler Approach

For example, I am grateful for my parents who paid for and allowed me to go on this trip and for my friends who made the day special, and of course, my protector who keeps a watchful eye over me. Without all of my mentions, I would never have experienced that day as I did and be grateful for the happy memory it has provided me with.

It is entirely up to you how you wish to express your gratitude and you may use different methods each time which is also highly suggested. Also, I'd like to mention that you may have your own unique ways of expressing gratitude in a way that feels best for you. Please continue to do what works for you. If you realise you are not feeling the happiness and joy from expressing gratitude that you once did, this may be an indication that you need to switch up the ways you are practicing gratitude. If you are struggling to feel sincerely grateful even after many attempts of practicing, this brings me to my **next point.**

Maybe

You need to heal

I am no doctor or psychiatrist. However, I am someone who has needed to heal from the past to move forwards and feel grateful for my present. I can still say that I am nowhere near where I would like to be but being aware of this is vitally important. With awareness, you can take the steps you need to. Unhealed pain, trauma, sadness, anger, or any other type of negative emotion that lives within you is a very persistent and powerful blocker in stopping you from feeling fully present and gracious for all that currently is. But the goal here is not to feel as though you must forget and have no emotions towards an experience but to recognise your negative thoughts and feelings to begin on your journey of healing with the end goal of feeling at peace.

"Let gratitude be the pillow upon which you kneel to say your nightly prayer. And let faith be the bridge you build to overcome evil and welcome good."

Maya Angelou

3 reasons why I am grateful for my family

1.
2.
3.

3 things that make me happy

1.
2.
3.

Draw something that you are grateful for

This week I am grateful for

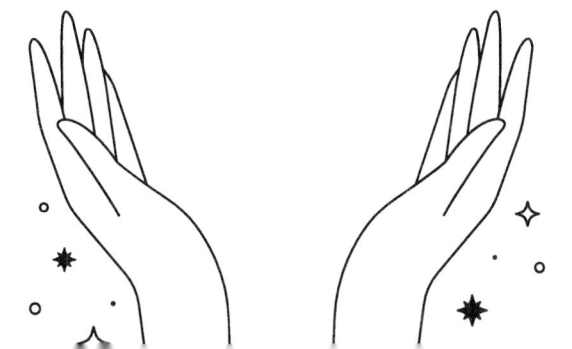

"Gratitude is an antidote to negative emotions, a neutralizer of envy, hostility, worry, and irritation. It is savoring; it is not taking things for granted; it is present-oriented."

Sonja Lyubomirsky

Did you know that, your brain is not you

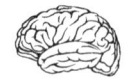

Gratitude cannot truly be felt if you continue to allow your brain to make your decisions for you. I can imagine you might have read that and thought 'But what do you mean allow my brain to make my decisions for me I have no control over my thoughts.'

Egyptian entrepreneur and writer Mo Gawdat shares how important it is to understand that you are not your brain and that you do not have to be a slave to every thought that your brain generates. For his equation of happiness, he explains that 'Gratitude is the ultimate solution to the happiness equation'. To remind yourself of what you're grateful for on a daily basis tells your brain, ok I know you're grumpy, I know you want to tell me the 7 things that went wrong today but your task right now is to go and find the thing that you're grateful for.

By implementing this gratitude reminder activity into your routine, suddenly your brain is searching and finding more things for you to be grateful for without being reminded because it's getting really good at it and life is full of blessings. He says this to be the absolute answer. Gawdat also has a concept he calls 'The Look Down' method. If the guy with 5 cars compares to the guy with 18 he will feel miserable. If the model compares to the supermodel she will feel miserable.

If you compare to the guy In Afghanistan or the girl in Syria or the family in the refugee camp you would suddenly realise, Oh My God I am so blessed. Constantly looking up will never allow you to feel happy or satisfied with where you are in life so just look down. Think of your mind like your digestive system — what you put in it impacts how you feel. When you flood your mind with a constant flow of worry, envy, resentment, and self-criticism (compounded by a barrage of news and other media) it negatively impacts your mental wellbeing.

A gratitude practice is like a workout and a healthy eating plan for your mind. In the article Why Gratitude is Good written by Dr. Emmons, he shares "You can't feel envious and grateful at the same time. They're incompatible feelings because if you're grateful, you can't resent someone for owning things you don't." He goes on to share that his research found that people with high levels of gratitude have low levels of resentment and envy. When we take time to focus on what we are grateful for, we choose positive emotions over negative, thus we take steps to nurture our mental health and wellbeing.

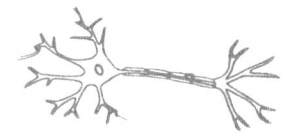

"Be grateful for what you already have while you pursue your goals. If you aren't grateful for what you already have, what makes you think you would be happy with more."

Roy T. Bennett

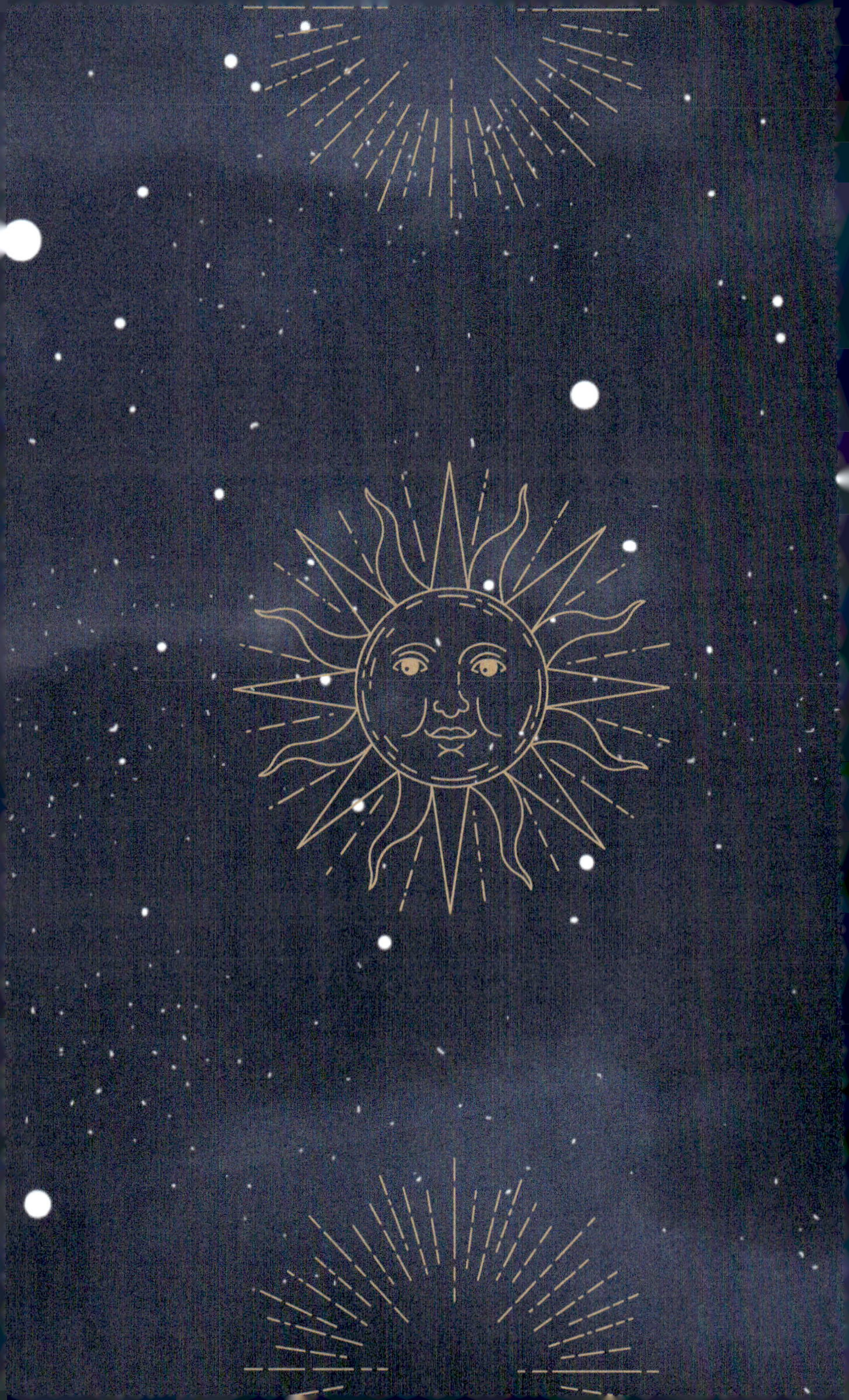

"Do not spoil what you have by desiring what you have not; remember that what you now have was once among the things you only hoped for."

EPICURUS

Earlier in the book, you wrote about an experience that forced you to grow which helped you shape into the person that you are today.

I would like you to repeat that exercise and write down another experience that forced you to grow, as I for one have plenty of experiences that forced me to grow and I'm sure you do too.

An experience that forced me to grow is when

I am grateful for this experience because

*For my last and final gratitude entry
I would like to say that I am most grateful for*

I would like to thank you for showing gratitude for all the good in your life, but most importantly you should thank yourself for taking the time to show gratitude for all the things you have and all that is to come. There may be things that you are not grateful for today that you may be grateful for in the future. Don't rush or force yourself to feel things you aren't yet ready to. Concentrate on the good, and in return, more good will come.

From this day on, may you live your life with gratitude always in mind until next time

Much Love,

Diana

you did it, how does it feel?

"Enjoy the little things, for one day you may look back and realize they were the big things."

Robert Brault

About the Author

Diana Playa is the owner of affordable luxury fashion brand **Le Playa** and runs a podcast called **The Girl Guide**. In her free time she loves to design sustainable womenswear, read and write books, and enjoy long walks in the park to catch the sunset.

Her mission is to spread awareness on topics she feels can help women and girls on their journeys just as they've helped her. She designs unique pieces for women to wear and feel liberated in and continues to encourage others on her podcast to be unapologetically themselves and live with no regrets.

@Dianaplaya
@Leplaya_
@Thegirlguide.xo

www.leplaya.co.uk
anchor.fm/thegirlguide

"Gratitude unlocks the fullness of life. It turns what we have into enough, and more. It turns denial into acceptance, chaos to order, confusion to clarity. It can turn a meal into a feast, a house into a home, a stranger into a friend."

Melody Beattie